REAL ESTATE SYNDICATOR'S MANUAL AND GUIDE

REAL ESTATE
SYNDICATOR'S
MANUAL AND GUIDE

MARTIN HUSSANDER

PRENTICE-HALL, INC.,
ENGLEWOOD CLIFFS, NEW JERSEY

PRENTICE-HALL INTERNATIONAL, INC., *London*
PRENTICE-HALL OF AUSTRALIA, PTY. LTD., *Sydney*
PRENTICE-HALL OF CANADA, LTD., *Toronto*
PRENTICE-HALL OF INDIA PRIVATE, LTD., *New Delhi*
PRENTICE-HALL OF JAPAN, INC., *Tokyo*

© 1969 BY

PRENTICE-HALL, INC.

ENGLEWOOD CLIFFS, N. J.

LIBRARY OF CONGRESS
CATALOG CARD NUMBER: 69–10508

PRINTED IN THE UNITED STATES OF AMERICA
B & P

ABOUT THE AUTHOR

Martin Hussander has been an active real estate operator for over thirty-five years. During his career, he has successfully syndicated more than fifty commercial buildings and residential developments. In the thirties and forties, he was Vice President of Albin J. Liepold, Inc., a Chicago-based real estate management firm, and a partner of its successor, Albin J. Liepold & Company. After moving to the West Coast in 1947, he became a licensed apartment and commercial contractor and subsequently a real estate broker. Mr. Hussander is now President of Almart, Inc., a commercial real estate syndicate headquartered in Santa Barbara, California.

For Pauline

What This Book Will Do for You

A study of the *Real Estate Syndicator's Manual and Guide* will make it possible for you to become a real estate syndicator. As a real estate syndicator you can make fantastic profits for yourself and for those who join your syndicate group to invest their capital for profit.

Step by step, this book provides detailed information concerning the activities which you would conduct as a real estate syndicator, and describes the operation of various types of real estate syndicates.

The information which I have assembled here has been taken from my own experience in the syndication of a large number of properties, ranging in size from small apartment buildings to medium-large apartment and commercial buildings as well as other types of real estate. The examples given have been taken from true situations in which I have been involved or of which I had personal knowledge.

This book tells you of the unusual profits which you can make, what types of real estate to syndicate, factors favorable to forming a real estate syndicate, how to select the type of organization to use, and how to form it. It provides detailed directions for the promotion, formation, operation, division of profits, and the dissolution of a real estate syndicate.

You may have had experience with subjects which are covered in this book, and for you, these sections will be valuable confirmation of your knowledge and capability. In your case the *Real Estate Syndicator's Manual and Guide* will fill the gaps and make it possible for you to become a real estate syndicator.

You will find that this book is primarily designed to furnish a clear picture of the operation of so called "private" real estate syndicates. This is a subject about which little has previously been written, because syndicators who operate "private" syndicates do not seek publicity, and do not make public offering of participating interests in their ventures.

The *Real Estate Syndicator's Manual and Guide*, therefore, opens up a wide new range of activity for you. With knowledge gained from this book you will know how to organize a "private" real estate syndicate which will pool the capital of participating investors, which group, with your guidance, will share the profit to be made from the venture.

You can be the syndicator who organizes a real estate syndicate, and you will then be able to control property with little or no investment of your own. The text and examples will show you how you can be well rewarded for your efforts as syndicator while paying very low taxes on your profits and earnings.

You will learn how other syndicators convince participating investors to join a real estate syndicate, which provides them with a safe, profitable investment and tax advantages.

With the information contained in this book you can become a real estate syndicator and form your own syndicate groups of investors. You will then share in the large profits to be made by applying the knowledge obtained from a study of *The Real Estate Syndicator's Manual and Guide*.

Chapter 1 tells you of the fantastic profits which have been made by means of group buying of real estate, wherein a syndicator provides the "know how" while a group of participating investors furnish the capital to buy the equity in the property.

This chapter also points out that a group of investors, guided by an expert syndicator, can own property large enough to employ expert property management, and that the participating investors in a real estate syndicate can enjoy tax advantages, make capital gains, and get profit from rents.

Further, the chapter outlines the benefits which accrue to the syndicator who guides the venture. He gets a share of total capital gains, rent income, possible real estate commissions and management income, as well as tax advantages, all with "leverage," which means little or no investment on his part.

Chapter 2 describes the main types of real estate which are suitable for real estate syndication. It includes an explanation of how different types of property can produce benefits which fit the requirements of participating investors with various goals. The advantages and disadvantages of each type of property are recounted, so that a syndicator can match the property to be purchased for syndication with the objectives of the investing group.

Chapter 3 enumerates the factors favorable to forming a real estate syndicate. The essential factors are emphasized, and the other favorable factors, which could add to the essential factors to produce a fantastic deal, are included.

Chapter 4, "Laying The Groundwork," gives a rundown on how to make a beginning when organizing a real estate syndicate. This chapter shows how to smooth the pathway towards lining up a group of participating investors who will join in a real estate syndicate.

Chapter 5 advances the thinking of the syndicator into the field of preliminary organization. Each step in the planning of this phase of forming a real estate syndicate is detailed here.

Chapter 6 lists those who can furnish professional help to a syndicator, covers the scope of the work which can be done by them to help in the formation of a successful real estate syndicate, tells how to employ their services, and indicates how to determine what their charges will be.

Chapter 7 is involved with the vital field of finding and attracting investors. Methods of accomplishing this objective, which have brought success to others in the formation of real estate syndicates, are recited. Examples of the public relations jobs which other syndicators have done are a part of this chapter.

Chapter 8 describes the tools which can be used to convince prospective participating investors to join the group which the syndicator wishes to organize to form a real estate syndicate. The Sample Prospectus, which is the main feature of the chapter, is an exhibit in detail of the basic framework for the organization of a real estate syndicate. A pattern for a real estate syndication, based on this Sample Prospectus, should convince prospective investors of the merit of joining in such a venture when the opportunity is presented. This chapter encompasses one of the most important subjects in *The Real Estate Syndicator's Manual and Guide*.

Chapter 9 compares the various types of organization which can be used as the business vehicle for a real estate syndication. The advantages and disadvantages of each type of business organization, and of each method of holding title to syndicate-owned real estate are reviewed and discussed.

Chapter 10 is a guide which shows how to find the investment. This chapter contains all of the salient points of listing a property which is to be considered as an investment for real estate syndication.

Chapter 11 reveals the sources of trend indicators which support the judgement of a syndicator as to the time to buy real estate, while *Chapter 12* details the methods which can be used by a syndicator to obtain control of a property which is to be used as the investment of the real estate syndicate to be formed.

Chapter 13 summarizes the duties of the syndicator with reference to the management of the syndicate, and *Chapter 14* defines the scope of the management of syndicate real estate.

Chapter 15 gives examples of reports to investors. Completely detailed samples are exhibited to delineate this important public relations subject.

In *Chapter 16* the methods by which syndicators solve the problem of how to increase the value of property are specified.

Chapter 17 outlines the factors which limit the holding period for syndicate-owned real estate, and *Chapter 18* provides guidelines to be followed in determining the selling price of real estate owned by a syndicate group.

The selling campaign is sketched in *Chapter 19*, which is illustrated with examples of descriptive property statements and plats of property to be sold. Pointers are given as to how to merchandise the resale of syndicate-owned real estate.

Chapter 20, "Dividing The Profits," marks the conclusion of a real estate syndicate transaction. Complete reporting of the closing of sample deals, computation of total profits made and of the sharing of profits by participating investors and syndicator is worked out. The tax benefits which accrue to the syndicate members are featured.

The Real Estate Syndicator's Manual and Guide provides information in depth covering all of the key subjects which will enable the reader to become a real estate syndicator. With use of the knowledge gained, a syndicator can make the profits which this rewarding field of activity offers.

ACKNOWLEDGMENT

I am indebted to my long-time partner, Albin J. Liepold, who has been associated with me in many real estate syndicates and who has unfailingly contributed his knowledge of real estate, his skills and his capabilities toward achieving our goals.

His support, and the experiences in real estate which we had together, enabled me to write this book.

Contents

DIVIDING THE PROFITS (Continued)

records for closing out organization. Prepare reports for syndicate members. Prepare tax returns for syndicate members. Pay out all funds according to syndicate agreement and then dissolve organization.

Complete all syndicate transactions. Review of organizational agreement with accountant. Secure escrow closing statements. Prepare accounting records for closing out organization. Prepare reports for syndicate members. Prepare tax return for syndicate. Pay out all funds according to syndicate agreement and dissolve organization.

REAL ESTATE SYNDICATOR'S MANUAL AND GUIDE

CHAPTER 1—

The Fantastic Profits of

Syndication

A "syndicate" is a body of persons who combine to carry through some financial transaction, or who undertake some common venture. Syndicates are often formed to acquire real estate, hold it for a short time and then resell it. The profits are then distributed and the syndicate dissolves.

A "syndicator" is one who syndicates; one who controls a syndicate.

A syndicate is a very flexible business arrangement which can be used to accomplish a number of different objectives.

MY FIRST SYNDICATE

The first real estate syndicate with which I was involved as a syndicator came about because of the sale of two twenty-four-apartment buildings. The real estate firm with which I was connected made the deal, but neither buyer or seller would pay a commission for making the deal. The buyer offered to sell an older twelve-apartment building at a very low price in lieu of commission.

Without sufficient funds to buy the twelve-apartment building, my partner and I were forced to sell shares in the building to our friends. We retained a 25 percent interest in the building with no investment of our own. We remodeled the building, doubled the rents, financed it, and then sold it to make a 215 per cent profit on money invested. This transaction convinced me that real estate syndication was good business.

THREE SUCCESSFUL SYNDICATES

Shortly after the sale of the twelve-apartment building, other opportunities were presented which appealed to us as syndicators, and for which we had an eager group of participating investors.

Within one year four or more properties were controlled by syndicates in which I was one of the syndicators. Each syndicate consisted of myself and partner as syndicators, and from six to ten participating investors who put up most of the capital to fund the syndicate.

The Logan Apartments, consisting of thirty-apartment units, all leased, was purchased, cleaned up, and painted on the exterior, held for about ten months and then sold to make a capital gain of 44.4 per cent on capital invested.

As syndicators, we got a subordinated 25 per cent interest in the capital gain profit. In this and in most subsequent deals, we also invested our own money for a share, which was treated the same as that of any other participating investor.

The Logan Apartments, fully rented, earned a 12 per cent net return, which was divided, according to agreement, while the property was held. Our management firm managed the property for a percentage of the gross rent collections, and we were paid brokerage commisssions on the purchase and sale of the syndicate property.

We paid nothing for our 25 per cent interest in the profit to be made from the deal, but our participating group was very happy with their investment, which was their only contribution to the venture.

A fifteen apartment building, bought from a large life insurance company at about the same time as the Logan Apartments purchase, brought a 73.3 percent capital gain in addition to rent income while holding the property. The seller had made a very favorable mortgage on the property, which helped with the resale. We had the same syndicator deal on the fifteen-apartment Eastwood Avenue building.

The 2800 East Main Street, Ventura, California, building, which is used as an example of a building which might have been syndicated at the resale price, was built by a small syndicate of which I was a member.

My partner and I designed the building, rented it, financed it, and sold it at a price of $175,000, which produced a capital gain of approximately 65 per cent after expenses of sale. While holding the property, we got a net income of about 15 per cent, considering the rent lost before the stores were all rented. We did not participate in the real estate commissions, and we employed a general contractor to build the building.

The 2800 East Main Street property was sold in order to go into another deal, so the sale price of $175,000 would have been attractive to another syndicator because of the fine net return of approximately 10 per cent with "cash flow" of almost 12 per cent. A full descriptive statement of the 2800 East Main Street building is shown in Chapter 8.

$100,000 CAPITAL GAIN FROM A ONE-STORY COMMERCIAL

Another syndicator of my acquaintance bought a strip of land on the parking lot of a large chain grocery store for $25,000. He then sold a half interest in the property to a building contractor for $25,000, leaving the first party with no cash investment. The building contractor was said to have sold half of his interest for $25,000.

This group, as a sort of spontaneous syndicate, then constructed a one-story commercial building with eleven small stores, each of which was rented to a tenant in a service business—launderette, cleaner, shoe repair, paints, barber, etc. The design of the building was simple, the cost only about $75,000. Gross annual rents exceeded $30,000.

This property was sold to produce over $200,000 net to the sellers. The total capital gain was about $100,000. There had been substantial rent income during the eighteen months that the syndicate had held the property.

This is how the $100,000 capital gain was divided:

a. The first syndicator got a $50,000 gain with no investment.

b. The building contractor made $25,000 with no money invested. He also made a contractor's profit on the construction.

c. The other members of the syndicate made a profit of $25,000, a 100 per cent gain on their investment of $25,000.

All members of the group shared in the rent income while holding the property.

Such profits are possible by means of "private" syndication of real estate when the deal is carefully planned and well managed, and when the resale of the property is properly merchandised.

I have been one of the syndicators in a large number of small- to medium-sized real estate syndicates. The profits ranged from 15 per cent to more than double the invested capital. Some of the smaller properties produced the greatest percentage of gains, but the syndicator's work was about the same as with a larger deal. The medium-sized deal, which is big enough to pay for expert management and advice, seems to be the best bet for a syndicator to work with.

These are the elements which combine to produce the fantastic profits for those who participate in a real estate syndicate as investors and syndicators.

FACTORS FAVORING THE PARTICIPATING INVESTOR

- The syndicator is a specialist
- A syndicate can own property large enough to employ expert management
- A real estate syndicate has tax advantages
- A syndicate can make capital gains
- A syndicate can make profits from rents

THE SYNDICATOR'S BENEFITS

- The syndicator gets a share of capital gains made by the syndicate
- He gets a share of the rent income
- He gets tax advantages
- He has "leverage"

- He gets management income
- He has potential real estate brokerage income

The syndicator is a specialist

A syndicator is trained to invest other people's money in real estate for their benefit. His knowledge, skill and capabilities are directed toward producing income, capital gain, tax advantage, or all three for those who join him in a real estate syndicate.

The syndicator gathers a group of participating investors together to purchase real estate which has been carefully selected to produce the desired benefits. He has a format which shows exactly how the invested capital will be used, what share of the profits will go to the investor, and how much will be paid to the syndicator for his share in the venture.

The average person who might invest money in a real estate syndicate does not have sufficient capital to buy a property which could command the attention of a specialist like the syndicator. Should this person buy a building for himself, he faces all the management and maintenance problems personally.

The party who invests capital in a syndicate to purchase real estate joins a group of persons who, together, can get the services of the syndicator's special qualifications.

The successful syndicator knows how to achieve his objectives. It is his business to operate real estate profitably. The syndicator is a specialist, and this makes his services valuable to a participating investor in a real estate syndicate.

A real estate syndicate has tax advantages

The participating investor in an acreage or vacant land deal can convert high earned income received in one year into long-term, low-taxed income in a subsequent year. Prepayment of interest and charging the expense of carrying vacant land against the investor's high, earned, ordinary income, in the year in which the expenses are paid out, produces this tax saving. An investor who participates in an *income property* syndicate gets to charge his share of the depreciation on the building against personal ordinary income, giving him "tax shelter."

A syndicate can make capital gains

A real estate syndicate is a strong owner of real estate. The group which makes up a real estate syndicate is able to carry property long enough to resell it in a favorable market in order to make a long-term capital gain.

An income property syndicate can make profits from rents

A real estate syndicate which becomes the owner of income property buys it on the basis of its earning power. These earnings are divided among the members of the syndicate in accordance with the provisions of the syndicate agreement. An increase in the rents of the building, which builds up the net income, allows for increased distributions of cash to the syndicate members, and raises the value of the property.

THE SYNDICATOR'S BENEFITS

The syndicator gets a share of the capital gains

The syndicator has the syndicate agreement drawn to provide a share of the capital gain for him when the syndicate-owned real estate is resold. The amount of the syndicator's share depends on the agreement. Usually the syndicator pays little or nothing for his share in the syndicate profits. Subordination of his share in the capital gain to the repayment of capital contributions made by the participating investors gives the syndicator capital gain tax treatment on this profit.

A syndicator could invest capital of his own on the same basis as the other participating investors. Profit from this interest in the syndicate would not be subordinated to the repayment of capital contributions of the other participating investors unless so provided in the agreement.

The syndicator gets a share of the rent income

The syndicator who organizes an *income property* syndicate provides in the syndicate agreement that he is to get a share of the net income earned by the property. The syndicator's share of net income from the property is usually subordinated to the payment of a certain return to the participating investors, so that they receive a priority up to a certain amount of the net income *before* the syndicator gets paid anything.

The syndicator gets tax advantages

Subordination of the syndicator's share of capital gain, if properly provided for in the syndicate agreement, makes it possible for him to treat any such profit as a long-term gain for income tax purposes.

The syndicator provides in the agreement that he is to get a share of the depreciation taken on improvements of income property owned by his syndicate. This depreciation can be charged against the syndicator's ordinary income to reduce tax.

The syndicator has "leverage"

The participating investor group, which contributes most or all of the capital needed to pay for the equity in syndicate-owned real estate, gives the syndicator practically a 100 per cent "leverage" situation. The syndicator controls the property with little or no investment of his own capital.

The syndicator gets management income

A syndicator contributes his expert management services, and he provides, in the Syndicate Agreement, that he is to be paid for such services. Some syndicators employ real estate management firms to handle these details, in which case the management fee is paid to that firm.

The syndicator has potential real estate brokerage income

A syndicator who is a real estate broker can make commissions when syndicate real estate is bought or sold, provided that he makes this arrangement in the Syndicate Agreement, and that his position is fully disclosed to all interested parties.

These are the elements which combine to produce fantastic profits for those who participate in a real estate syndicate, as participating investors, and as syndicators.

POINTS TO KEEP IN MIND

√ The syndicator is a professional who recognizes the growth potential of certain real estate. He can provide organizational skill, buying judgement, management ability and selling capability.

√ A real estate syndicate can get "tax shelter" and long term capital gain tax treatment.

√ Rents from income property can produce "tax sheltered" income while a real estate syndicate holds property for long term capital gain.

√ The syndicator gets a share of syndicate rent income, capital gains and tax advantages.

√ The syndicator not only has "leverage," but he also has potential income from management of the syndicate real estate and real estate brokerage.

These elements add up to make possible the fantastic profits of which I have spoken, and of which detailed examples can be found in this book.

Fantastic profits are there to be made by means of real estate syndication in any rising market. "Tight money" can be an advantage to a syndicator.

The background of successful real estate syndication is based on knowledge, perseverance, exposure, self-confidence, and a desire to make money. Application of these attributes supported by a study of this book, can bring you fantastic profits from real estate syndication.

CHAPTER 2—

What Types of Real Estate

to Syndicate

Determine the type of real estate to syndicate by following these guidelines:

- Study the three broad classifications of real estate, as described in this chapter, particularly directing attention to those features of each type which would make them attractive for syndication.
- Estimate the "leverage" possibilities of each type property.
- Define the objectives of the syndicator.
- Enumerate the benefits which appear to be required to attract inactive investors to join a real estate syndicate.
- Calculate, roughly, the amount of money which should be raised to syndicate property selected for syndication.
- Decide on the type and size of property to syndicate by matching desirable features of available properties to syndicator objectives, to the requirements of prospective syndicate members, and to the amount of money which can be expected to be raised by the syndication.

THE THREE BROAD CLASSIFICATIONS OF REAL ESTATE

I. *Acreage*, consisting of land suitable for agriculture or ranching, and rough land suitable for recreational uses, with possibilities of development of oil or mineral rights.

II. *Vacant land*, suited or zoned for homes, apartments, commercial, industrial or similar uses. Land on the fringe of rapid development.

7

III. *Improved real estate*, including homes, apartment, commercial, office and industrial buildings, or partly developed real estate.

I. ACREAGE

Acreage, by its very nature, lends itself to syndication for special purposes.

The main advantages to purchasing well selected acreage as property to syndicate are these:

1. Potential for capital gain.

2. Possibility of seller accepting—
   a. Prepaid interest, which attracts investors who wish to defer payment of ordinary income tax in very high earning years, converting deferred taxable income into favorably tax treated capital gain in a subsequent year.
   b. Installment sale with low down payment, say 10 per cent of purchase price and low annual payments on the balance. (*Advantage to buyer*—he pays out a small amount of his principal, with which he buys a large amount of acreage, taking a number of years to pay for it. *Advantage to seller*—he pays income tax only proportionately. Proportionate capital gain tax based on amount of cash paid on balance of purchase price each year).

3. Income tax deductions for purchaser. Expenses of carrying the property, including real estate taxes, interest, insurance and miscellaneous expense items, can be used to offset earned income of the purchaser while holding the land for future gain.

4. Possibility of special influences which could cause a sharp increase in the value of the acreage. These influences could include rezoning, discovery of oil or minerals on the land, the building of public improvements, roads, dams, parks, schools, the location of an industry or other advantageous private facility nearby, and many other influential occurrences and developments.

5. Minimum management problem while just sitting and waiting for a favorable market in which to resell the property.

Disadvantages of purchasing acreage are:

1. Income is usually little or nothing.

2. Difficult financing unless seller provides this. Financing unavailable from banks or recognized mortgage lenders.

3. Interest on the unpaid balance of purchase price, principal payments, real estate taxes, insurance and other expenses of holding the property will have to be paid. Syndicate members will have to be assessed to make these payments, if a syndicate is the purchaser.

4. Little or no "tax shelter."

5. Possible long holding period.

6. Difficulty of determining value.

An example of a syndicate purchasing acreage appeared as a news item in a Los Angeles newspaper recently. The details of this deal, as reported, point out some of the advantages which can accrue to the syndicate members. The essence of the deal, as reported, follows:

DOCTORS POOL TO BUY SONOMA RANCH SITE

"Group purchasing" may become a popular means of real estate investment, it appeared last week as thirty Los Angeles physicians reportedly combined with a land company to buy a 4,800-acre Sonoma County ranch.

The firm disclosed that it had formed a limited partnership with the doctors, all anesthesiologists, to acquire the property for $620,000.

It is situated near Healdsburg, seventy miles north of San Francisco, in the vicinity of a $70 million flood control project which will produce a fifteen-mile-long man-made lake, a spokesman said.

Roads to the lake, which will cover 3,300 acres, bisect the ranch property.

According to the land company, the Army Corps of Engineers plans to dam the conflux of Warm Springs and Dry Creeks, tributaries of the Russian River, northwest of Healdsburg.

It quoted the district chief as saying the dam will be 2,850 feet long by 284 feet high, and that the first construction contract probably will be let this summer.

Group purchasing is a relatively new plan in large acreage buys, but a very practical one, an official of the land investment firm commented.

"Small investors may pool comparatively modest amounts and, collectively, obtain all the advantages of a major purchase," he said, adding:

"Thus they are able to obtain better and larger properties at a lower price per acre, as well as the legal and financial benefit of a limited partnership."

He said studies are under way for proposed development of the property into two and a half to forty-acre sites.

Note that this news item has covered most of the "advantages" which I attributed to the purchase of acreage, namely:

Item 1. Potential for capital gain.

Item 2. Expenses of carrying property offset large earned income of purchaser.

Item 3. Special influences to boost values, plus division into smaller parcels for later resale at higher prices.

Item 4. Management—the land company syndicator does this.

The article did not disclose the financing details, although "prepaid interest" and an "installment sale" could have been a part of the arrangement. A syndicate this large, with thirty doctors involved, should have been able to pay cash for the ranch if that had been desirable to meet its requirements.

Conclusion: Acreage has great merit for syndication purposes when it can be used to the advantage of the syndicate members.

II. VACANT LAND

Vacant Land is suited or zoned for homes, apartments commercial or industrial uses. It is land on the fringe of rapid development.

This type of property has many of the same characteristics which apply to acreage, but it also has added advantages in that it is ready for development. It is on the fringe of real estate which is already improved, and it is undoubtedly zoned for a particular use, such as for apartments or for commercial or industrial uses.

The main advantages to purchasing well-selected vacant land are these:

1. Potential for capital gain.
2. Possibility of seller accepting—
   a. Prepaid interest (same advantages as for acreage).
   b. Installment sale with low down payment and low annual installments on the balance of the purchase price (advantages same as with acreage).
3. Expenses of property, taxes, interest, etc., can be used to offset a large earned income of purchaser—a deduction to reduce income tax at high ordinary rates while waiting for a resale in a favorable market to make a profit at low capital gain rates of income tax.
4. Possibility of special influences which could cause a great increase in the value of the vacant land, such as construction of public improvements, including streets and underground improvements, public buildings, bridges, dams, etc. Large private building in the area—residences, commercial and industrial, rezoning of property for more intensive use, and other influences.
5. Minimum management problem; just sit and wait for a favorable market.

Vacant land usually has a number of other advantages which are important to a syndicate purchaser, such as:

6. Public improvements are usually in and paid for, including sewer, water, sidewalks and street lighting.
7. Public utilities are there, including electricity, gas and garbage collection.
8. The property is zoned for specified uses, with ascertainable restrictions.
9. Commercial and industrial land can produce some temporary income by renting it for the sale of automobiles, landscaping materials, parking, etc.

10. Vacant land is ready for development.

11. Development of surrounding land by others—the "growth factor"—accelerates the potential for capital gains.

The additional advantages of vacant land over acreage are valuable, and they cost money when the land is purchased.

Disadvantages of purchasing vacant land for syndication are:

1. Income is usually little or nothing (except as noted in "advantages").

2. Difficult financing unless seller provides financing. Financing from banks or recognized lenders is difficult to get.

3. Taxes, interest and expenses will have to be paid while holding the property. Syndicate members will have to be assessed to meet these payments.

4. Little or no "tax shelter."

5. Holding period could be a long one.

6. Difficulty of determining value (vacant land is much more easily valued than acreage, but true values can vary widely on parcels which are just a short distance apart).

There are other disadvantages to purchasing vacant land for syndication, for instance:

7. When the land is held over two years, the carrying charges can eat up all of the potential profit. Interest, taxes and other expense could easily amount to 10 per cent a year on the entire purchase price, and this carrying cost compounds annually. A natural price rise of 3 per cent a year (inflation), can be expected as average, so it is obvious that "special influences" would have to be effective to pick up the rest of the carrying costs and to provide a profit.

Residential vacant land for home building, and any other land which is subdivided to be sold in individual lots is subject to ordinary income tax when sold. The only way that a syndicate could take advantage of the favorable capital gains tax would be to acquire the land, get tentative subdivision map approval, then sell off sizable portions of the tract at a time and let the buyer do the actual subdividing.

Well selected vacant land does have a tremendous capital gain potential, and, in addition, the development possibilities are many and profitable with the right conditions prevailing. A well-thought-out development of land by construction of buildings on it could convert the project into a very profitable income producer instead of a continuing expense.

Land is the type of real estate which has consistently shown the greatest potential for capital growth. Urban land on the periphery of metropolitan areas has advanced in price more rapidly than any other type of real estate. Generally, land has risen in price faster than any other form of property, including securities.

It is my opinion that commercial land has been the outstanding performer, industrial land a close follower, with residential land increasing in price at a more moderate rate. In many areas the price of developing urban land has risen at a rate which is double or triple that of stocks. Land has no peer as a hedge against inflation.

Financing land is not easy. Banks and mortgage lenders do not favor loans on vacant land. A purchaser of land must usually look to the seller for financing, and to face paying cash on some monthly or annual arrangement.

Vacant land usually yields no income, or very little income. The purchaser must be able to pay taxes, interest, insurance, principal payments and other expenses as these become due.

Vacant land requires a minimum of management, a real point in favor of this type of property as an investment. A land purchaser, seeking capital gain, merely gets control of the property and then just waits for the right market in which to resell at a profit.

Conclusion: Vacant land can be outstanding as an investment for a real estate syndicate, especially if the syndicate members have large earned incomes. Active areas in California, and in many other areas of the country show profits up to 100 per cent or more for land investors when values have skyrocketed due to growth pressures.

III. IMPROVED REAL ESTATE

Improved real estate, with the exception of homes, presents an entirely different aspect for the consideration of the syndicator. This type of property, when rented, is a going business.

Valuation of an income property which is fully improved can be determined by calculating the net return on cash invested, by figuring out the "cash flow," and comparing this with other offerings, and with the benefits which are required by other buyers to induce them to buy property of similar type.

"Cash flow" can be distributed to those who join a syndicate, and "tax shelter" defers at least a part of their ordinary income tax, which is converted into preferred long-term gain treatment when the property is sold.

The growth factor is limited, however, by the returns demanded by the buyers at the time of resale, which in turn is gauged by the demand for the type of property to be sold.

The purchase of partly developed improved real estate offers some present income to support the unimproved part of the property, and provides the opportunity of adding additional buildings which should produce a developer's high return to add to that which the property is already earning.

A syndicate organized with the purpose of developing vacant land by erecting buildings on it can make large profits. There are many risks to this sort of project, including the feasibility of the deal, the planning, financing and supervising of construction, and the problems of successfully renting the space. A syndication of property on which the improvements are to be built should be tried only by an experienced promoter who provides safeguards against the pitfalls which can beset such a development.

Conclusion: Probably the safest type of property to syndicate is that which is already improved and rented, with a predictable income, and expenses which can be determined by experience and an inspection of records of the seller. I recommend that a syndicator who is just starting out should try income property for his first syndication.

The main advantages of syndicating improved property are these:

1. There should be net income and "cash flow" for distribution to those who join the syndicate.

2. There will be "tax shelter" to defer payment of tax on part of the cash distributions to syndicate members, and to convert this tax to capital gain tax when the property is resold.

3. Depreciation on improvements creates "tax shelter."

4. Potential for capital gain (limited by net return on investment at time of resale).

5. Possibility of seller accepting:

   a. Prepaid interest (not very important since depreciation gives income "tax shelter").

   b. Installment sale with low down payment and low annual installments on the balance of the purchase price (advantages same as with acreage).

   c. Secondary financing with interest only and no payments on the principal for a reasonable time.

6. Possibility of special influences which could cause an increase in the value of the property, such as public improvements, large building activity in area with consequent increased population, increases in rents, reductions in expenses, rezoning, or other influences.

7. Income from property pays for professional management of the real estate (an advantage for the syndicator, who should be compensated for this service).

8. Income to pay for competent legal and accounting advice.

9. Pride of ownership.

Disadvantages of syndicating improved property are:

1. Management is necessary and must be paid for.

2. Competent legal, accounting and tax advice is needed and must be paid for.

3. Potential for capital gain is limited by the returns required to induce a buyer to purchase the property at the time it is to be resold.

4. Neighborhood changes must be carefully watched.

I point out that there are areas where certain types of property do not exist. For instance, industrial property could be the one which is not available in your locale, or possibly acreage is too far away to be of interest.

Choose a type of real estate that is in the area of interest, match it to syndicator objectives, and to the requirements of prospective members of the syndicate.

How to estimate the "leverage" possibilities

"Leverage" possibilities should be estimated so as to be able to gauge the amount of money to be raised by syndication in order to pay for the equity in the property to be purchased.

Estimate the "leverage" possibilities this way:

1. Watch the real estate transfers and recording of mortgages, or go to the county recorder's office and look up recent transfers and mortgage recordings. Ask at the recorder's office if the true equity is reflected by subtracting the recorded mortgage from the recorded sales price as indicated by the revenue stamps on the deed.

2. Inquire of real estate brokers. They can usually tell the percentage of cash needed to purchase equities in various types of real estate.

3. Inquire of lenders. These inquiries should give you a background from which to estimate the amount of cash which must be raised to purchase a property in the price bracket selected.

A San Francisco attorney specializing in real estate recently told me that a 25 per cent equity was considered to be conservative when related to purchase of larger apartment buildings in that city. This would indicate that a syndicate which could raise $100,000 could purchase a property which cost $400,000 or more.

"Leverage" can be a determining factor in the size of property to syndicate, and the availability of financing can be so different with the various types of real estate that "leverage" could also determine the type of real estate to syndicate.

How to define the syndicator's objectives

Just set down the benefits which you, as a syndicator, could expect to get by forming a real estate syndicate. Choose the ones which are most desirable to you, within the range of possibility. This will limit the types of property which can be considered for syndication, since some of the benefits can be had only when dealing with a particular type of property.

The benefits which a syndicator might expect to get are as follows:

1. A share of the syndicate in exchange for assigning the contract to purchase the property. This share can be subordinated to the shares of those who

make a cash contribution to the venture when they join, and, if the syndicate agreement is properly drawn, the syndicator's interest can be tax free at time of acquisition.

2. A cash profit when the contract to purchase the property is assigned to the syndicate.

3. A subordinated share of the "cash flow."

4. A real estate manager's fee.

5. Real estate brokerage commissions.

6. A leaseback of the property to syndicator at rent which could produce a profit by subleasing.

7. "Leverage" for the syndicator.

Suppose the syndicator has plenty of ordinary income and wants to make a capital gain? This syndicator could consider acreage or vacant land to syndicate.

Current income can be obtained for the syndicator only by syndicating income property, so, if this is the objective, then income property it must be.

Benefits which attract inactive investors

Sound out the syndicate prospects, those who might want to join a real estate syndicate, to ascertain their desires. Undoubtedly they will be attracted by the benefits enumerated.

1. A return on their money, larger than they can get from stocks or in a bank
2. "Tax shelter," to defer income tax and convert to capital gain later
3. Reasonable safety of principal
4. A possibility of capital gain
5. Pride of ownership
6. Capable and reliable management with no effort by them

The investors who desire these benefits would have interest in a real estate syndication of income property.

Those investors who want to invest in futures, deferring income tax in high earning years, would be interested in a real estate syndicate dealing with acreage or vacant land.

How to calculate the amount of money which can be raised for a syndicate

Make a list of friends, relatives and associates who are most likely to want to join in a real estate syndicate. Decide what their interests would be. Is it capital gain, deferred income, or present income? Make a guess as to how much each would contribute to a real estate venture. Are there ten prospects who might each invest $10,000, or maybe twenty who would put in $5,000 each?

These estimates of the amount of capital which can be raised determine the size project which can be considered. If $100,000 can be raised, with a 25 per cent equity, the syndicate can handle property which costs up to $400,000.

When "laying the groundwork" a closer calculation of the amount of capital available for syndication will be possible.

POINTS TO KEEP IN MIND

√ The type of real estate chosen to be syndicated must produce the advantages required to attract participating investors.

√ "Leverage" potential is important but not essential to a successful real estate syndication.

√ The syndicator must estimate the capital which can be raised by syndication of various types of real estate.

√ The syndicator's profit opportunities should be arranged to his satisfaction.

√ The size of the project should be matched to the estimated capital to be raised by syndication.

CHAPTER 3—

Factors Favorable to Forming

A Real Estate Syndicate

These are the eleven factors favorable to forming a real estate syndicate:

**An active real estate market with rising prices.
  •Satisfactory returns from income property.
**Potential for capital gain.
  •No management problems for inactive investors.
  •"Tax shelter."
**Limited liability for inactive investors.
  •"Leverage."
  •Benefits from purchasing a larger property.
**Availability of prospective syndicate members.
  •"Special influences."
**The syndicator.

**These are critical factors which must always be present before deciding to form a real estate syndicate. The remaining six factors can be very important, but they need not be present in every case.

An active real estate market with rising prices

This is a factor which cannot be overlooked when considering the formation of a real estate syndicate. An "active market" is caused by many of the other factors favorable to forming a real estate syndicate, so that the indications that these influences are supporting the market are of great importance to a syndicator.

The manifestations of an active real estate market are there for an alert observer to see. Real estate transfers are a gauge of the volume of transactions, and revenue stamps on deeds can reveal the sale prices. Comparison with previous sales of the same property shows the trend, with real estate assessments confirming it. Assessor's records also disclose the activity of the market, divulge the name of the owner of the property, and give the assessed valuation of the land and building.

A Los Angeles newspaper recently published a "Box Score of Southern California Growth." This contained a wealth of information valuable to a syndicator. San Diego County stood out as the one making the most progress at the time. Such an indication of growth, which contributes to an active real estate market with rising prices, would command the attention of syndicators, and attract them to the San Diego area as a base of operations.

A "box score" must be carefully interpreted, however. Localities which are presently making excellent progress might have made a phenomenal spurt forward in the previous year of comparisons. The "box score" would then show a drop in the rate of growth which could be deceptive and disenchant some owners. These owners might then be willing to sell their property at a bargain price, which would present a real opportunity for an astute syndicator.

An active real estate market with rising prices is essential to the success of a syndicate which is to be formed, but I must point out that there are degrees of activity. The degree of activity in the locale where syndicate activity is contemplated might be eminently satisfactory for the purposes of the syndicate, and still not be top in a "box score." Analyze the data carefully, then make the decisions which fit the circumstances.

Satisfactory returns from income property

The real estate syndicator who intends to attract members to join his group, and to attract them with a relatively large return on the capital outlay which they make, must be concerned with the net income and "cash flow" of the properties to be considered for syndication.

Well-selected income property earns more per dollar invested than the same capital would earn if invested in stocks, bonds or other business investments.

"Cash flow," the amount available for distribution to investors in a real estate syndicate, can easily be as much as eight to ten per cent or more on cash invested in the venture. Equity buildup, the principal payments made on mortgages out of building income, often adds another two to three per cent a year to net income.

Syndicated income real estate, professionally managed, produces an amount of net income which cannot be matched elsewhere. The distributions which can be made in cash from the income provide a powerful attraction to investors, showing that satisfactory returns from income property constitute a powerful factor favoring formation of a real estate syndicate.

Potential for capital gain—inflation hedge

The potential for capital gain is a strong factor favorable to forming a real estate syndicate.

Every mature real estate investor has his favorite story about the land which could have been bought a few years ago for a fraction of its present value.

Wealthy individuals, a great many of them from the entertainment world, have bought large tracts of real estate and have made sizeable gains while enjoying tax advantages. They have bought at lower prices per acre because they could handle the big deals which require a lot of capital, and they can pay the carrying charges on the property until the market price goes up.

A well-organized syndicate can do the same thing that the wealthy individual can do, and be safer while doing it. The very fact that there are a number of participants in a syndicate spreads the risk, as well as the cost of holding the property. A syndicate can be a very strong owner.

Well-selected acreage or vacant land can far outstrip "growth stocks" for capital gain potential, and in some instances the capital gain can be fantastic, far exceeding inflationary pressures.

Income property also has a fine capital gain potential, but the gain is limited by net income and "cash flow," balanced against the requirements of buyers who might consider the property.

An increase in rents could increase the net income of a property, and thus increase the value of it.

A few years ago, strip store commercial property in cities on the fringe of Los Angeles could be sold based on an eight per cent return on the full price of the property. Today, buyers of strip stores look for ten per cent net return on a clear building. In this market, then, every dollar of increased net income would boost the value of the building by $10. In the previous eight per cent market, a dollar of increased net income would add $12.50 to the value of the property.

The capital gain potential of income real estate is closely tied to net income, "cash flow" and the requirements of the prospective buyers of such property. Acreage or vacant land, on the other hand, could have a spectacular rise in price which buyers would pay, and have had no income at all.

Inflation affects all commodities, including real estate. It seems to be the general impression that the inflation effect is at the average rate of about three per cent a year. All commodities would seem to be attractive for those seeking an inflation hedge, and, if held long enough, this would undoubtedly hold true.

Inflation does not take effect at an average rate, however. Inflation affects the economy, and indeed affects individual commodities, in surges. Suddenly, the public becomes aware of the fact that increased labor and material cost have forced increases in the price of commodities, of which real estate is one.

Inflation is one of the influences which produces capital gain. One who buys real estate just prior to a surge of inflation benefits to a much greater degree than the average rate of inflation would indicate. This buyer will have already acquired his real estate, and when the public rushes into the market to protect itself against the effects of inflation, and the surge is exaggerated, prices advance radically, and the wise buyer who bought early makes a killing.

These facts of business life demonstrate that the potential for capital gain and built-in inflation hedge, which are qualities of real estate, exert a powerful influence on investors, and constitute a factor which favors the formation of real estate syndicates.

No management problems for inactive investors

Ownership of real estate usually poses management problems for the owner, and the smaller the property, the more the owner becomes involved, even to the point of doing his own repairs and garden maintenance.

The party who joins a real estate syndicate as an inactive investor avoids all problems with relation to the management or maintenance of the property and of the syndicate.

Pooling his capital with that of other members of the real estate syndicate, an inactive investor is a part of a group which has a syndicator who manages the affairs of the syndicate, and the syndicator either manages the real estate which the syndicate owns, or employs the services of a managing real estate agent to do so.

This feature is one of the main attractions which induces investors to join real estate syndicates instead of individually owning smaller parcels of property.

The inactive investor in a real estate syndicate has liabilities and responsibilities which are no greater than they would be with the ownership of stock or other securities, yet the returns from participation in a real estate syndicate can be very much higher than those obtainable from other forms of investment. "Tax shelter" can reduce the income tax bite on this high return, a benefit not applicable to other forms of investment.

Investors are attracted to real estate syndicates because there are *no management problems for inactive investors,* a potent factor in favor of forming a real estate syndicate.

"Tax shelter"

"Tax shelter" is the reduction of income tax at ordinary rates by using the depreciation deduction on depreciable property to effectively reduce taxable income.

A syndicate can be set up to pass along a share of this depreciation deduction to each of the members of a real estate syndicate, so that they can use the deduction as it applies to their own personal income tax situation.

The real estate syndicate, pooling the capital of a group of investors, can purchase property which, by reason of the income derived therefrom, or by reason of the size of the deal, can command expert tax advice to get all the available "tax shelter" benefits.

"Tax shelter," then, would attract investors to join a real estate syndicate, and be a factor favorable to forming such a syndicate.

Limited liability for inactive investors

A real estate syndicate can be organized to provide limited liability for those who join it as inactive investors, and this is a feature which is desirable to all who invest money.

The corporate form of organization naturally comes to the mind of almost everyone who seeks limited liability, and, in some instances, this vehicle is suitable for syndication. The corporation furnishes limited liability to all classes of investors in it. Unfortunately the corporation does not ordinarily provide the tax advantages of other forms of business organization with relation to ownership of real estate.

The limited partnership form of organization lends itself well to real estate syndication, furnishing limited liability for the limited partners. The liability of general partners can be minimized to a satisfactory degree.

Investors look for "limited liability." This feature, when included as part of the organizational vehicle, is a forceful factor favoring the formation of a real estate syndicate.

"Leverage"

"Leverage" is a new term for an old device called limit financing. The "leverage" theory is that of borrowing other people's money at an interest rate which is lower than the rate of net income earned by the property which secures the loan. I have seen articles relating to the financing of real estate which contained recommendations that "leverage" be used to finance real estate to the extent of 100 to 110 per cent of value, if this could be accomplished. I do not believe that this is sound advice.

There are risks involved in owning an income property which is heavily mortgaged. If things go well, the owner of a property which employs maximum "leverage" makes a return which is far larger per dollar of equity investment than could be made with a more conservatively financed property. On the other hand, if rents drop or vacancies occur, the owner of the heavily "leveraged" property is in difficulty and might lose all of his invested capital.

Certainly there are risks in employing maximum "leverage" with relation to a syndicated property, risks which a wise syndicator would avoid, and which in some states would be prohibited.

"Leverage," employed with prudence, is a valuable tool of the syndicator. A syndicate can usually be considered to be a strong owner of real estate, and the combined resources of the members of the syndicate constititute a safety factor which is unique, and which can be counted on to carry a syndicated property until conditions again become favorable. "Leverage" can be very valuable for a syndicate, especially when the members of the syndicate are financially secure, are mature investors, and fully informed as to the risks involved.

"Leverage" for the syndicator is a different matter entirely. The participants, the inactive investors, furnish the "leverage" for the syndicator. They furnish the equity money; the syndicator furnishes the knowledge, management, organizational ability, in fact all of the other elements of a successful operation. The syndicator's "leverage" might be 100 per cent, and yet the syndicate deal could be conservatively financed with only a reasonable business risk for the inactive investors who have joined him.

"Leverage," used with prudence, is a valuable factor favoring the formation of a real estate syndicate.

Benefits from purchasing a larger property

Think of ten individuals, each investing $10,000 in a separate property. These individual properties would be small, because $10,000 would probably only purchase the equity in a duplex, or some other small property valued at $30,000 to $40,000.

Each of these individual owners would have all of the problems which face the owner of a larger property. A single vacancy constitutes a loss of 50 per cent of gross income, so these owners must be so concerned when this happens that they spend their leisure time waiting for prospective tenants. These owners usually have to do their own maintenance work on the building, keep their own records, and make tax returns.

Now, suppose that these ten investors join a real estate syndicate, and each gets a partial interest in a larger property for his $10,000 of capital. By pooling their capital they now would have $100,000 to invest, and this amount would purchase the equity in property valued at $300,000 or more.

Management problems are solved by the syndicator, who operates the syndicate affairs and manages the real estate or hires management of it.

The syndicator is a specialist in the purchase of property, management of it, and formation and management of the real estate syndicate. He is operating a property large enough to command his attention, and the revenue from the property pays for employment of competent legal and tax advice. The syndicator's compensation is dependent on a profitable operation of the syndicate. The owners of small properties could not afford to hire the services which a syndicator can render.

Who could deny that the *benefits from purchasing a larger property* are a factor favoring formation of a real estate syndicate?

Availability of prospective syndicate members

No one could fail to recognize that the formation of a syndicate requires that there be prospective syndicate members available (see Chapter 7).

When you have found these interested people, eager to join your syndicate, you will agree that the availability of prospective syndicate members is one of the principal factors favoring the formation of a real estate syndicate.

"Special influences"

"Special influences" may favor certain properties or types of properties, and the knowledge of these forces is extremely valuable to the syndicator.

Building of new roads, schools, residential developments, factories, water storage facilities, recreational areas, shopping facilities—any one of these could create a demand for surrounding property at increased prices, or higher rents.

Special influences can be outstanding as factors favoring the formation of a real estate syndicate.

The syndicator

The single most important factor favoring the formation of a real estate syndicate is the syndicator.

The knowledge, judgment and experience of the syndicator, (or the team of syndicators if there are more than one), fortified by a study of *Real Estate Syndicator's Manual and Guide*, can give an expert's touch to the formation of a real estate syndicate.

Confidence is generated among those who have money to invest in real estate and who find that the syndicator knows the techniques—how to organize a real estate syndicate, how to buy right, manage well and sell profitably when the time is right.

The syndicator, by pooling the capital of a number of investors, can acquire a larger property for the group than they could buy individually, making it possible to employ competent legal and tax advice, and to eliminate duplication of management and maintenance functions, which the syndicator supplies.

These capabilities on the part of the syndicator produce a carefree investment for inactive investors who have a relatively small amount of capital to invest, so that they will receive the high returns they seek, plus tax advantages. Without a syndicator there would be no syndicate.

POINTS TO KEEP IN MIND

√ A syndicator looks for a strong real estate market with values increasing.

√ He recognizes opportunities for capital gain.

√ The syndicator arranges his deal to give participating investors limited liability.

√ He attracts investors with capital to put into his venture.

√ The syndicator has real estate "know how" and uses it for the benefit of participating investors and himself.

√ He takes advantage of any other factors favorable to forming a real estate syndicate.

CHAPTER 4—

Laying the Groundwork

Laying the groundwork means just that and no more. Some call it "missionary work." The idea is to educate a group of prospective real estate syndicate investors so that they are familiar with the aims of the syndicator, with the format which will be used in forming the syndicate, with the security of their invested capital, and the returns which they might expect to get by investing in it.

The format will use as an example a description of a property which would fit into and measure up to the requirements of such a real estate syndicate, but the description is *not* that of a property which is to be syndicated.

Informing a group of people of an intention to form a real estate syndicate, telling them just how it is to be done, showing them a prospectus which includes details of a property which might be a worthwhile investment for such a syndicate, exhibiting the forms of agreement which will constitute the framework of the organizational vehicle which is to be used for the contemplated syndication—this is "laying the groundwork." Such activity is only educational and could not be interpreted as making an offering of any kind of securities, because the property of which details are given is *not* one which will be syndicated.

Laying the groundwork is one of the steps in the organization of any business venture, and is an activity which will be used when a preliminary organization is put together, and also prior to forming the syndicate itself.

There are several reasons for laying the groundwork as outlined and further detailed in this chapter.

One reason is that those people who might be interested in joining a real estate syndicate need education as to how it works, what the purposes are, what the returns can be, how returns will be divided, and what the liabilities and risks are.

Another reason would be that the syndicator would not want to disclose the particular property which is to be syndicated prior to the time when it is controlled and everything is set to go ahead with the syndication.

Further, the business law in various states is not uniform. There are some states in which a permit for public offering of limited partnership interests is not available. California is one of these states. Therefore care must be used to establish the fact that a real estate syndicate using a limited partnership agreement as a vehicle is a "private syndicate."

Participating interests in a giant eastern real estate syndicate were offered in only 32 states, which were probably the states which permitted such a public offering.

Therefore, laying the groundwork is educational only. It is an essential part of high-grade salesmanship. It gives prospective investors a chance to consider the setup, and then, if they are satisfied that it offers a good deal for them, they will be eager to join when a suitable property is found.

FOLLOW THIS PATTERN WHEN LAYING THE GROUNDWORK

- Make a list of prospective syndicate investors.
- Estimate the capital each prospect is expected to be able to contribute to a syndicate venture.
- Detail the syndicator's objectives.
- Use a preliminary prospectus—see Chapter 8.
- Contact prospective investors—inform them of intention of forming a real estate syndicate.
- Analyze prospect reaction, make format adjustments if appropriate.
- Proceed toward the goal selected.

Make a list of prospective syndicate investors

The list of prospects should include relatives, friends, business associates, in fact everyone who might have an interest in real estate as an investment, or in joining a real estate syndicate.

Go through address books, Christmas card lists, even the telephone book in smaller communities, in order to collect all the names of possible prospects, together with their addresses and telephone numbers.

The list which you compile is the source of participants in the contemplated real estate syndicate, and should be kept in a safe place.

Duplicate the prospect list on file cards, so that these cards can be arranged in alphabetical or other order as needed. Ruled 4" × 6" file cards serve well and leave room enough for the information which will be gathered about each of the prospects as time passes.

These cards are the working list of prospects to be taken into the field for contact work. The list kept at the office is insurance against losing the working cards.

Estimate the capital each prospect is expected to contribute to a syndicate venture

These estimates can only be guesses. Revisions will have to be made as prospects are contacted. Think big enough. Most people have more money to invest than they are credited with.

The estimation of the total amount of capital which might be raised for a real estate syndicate is the measure of the size property which the syndicate could handle.

One land syndicator of my acquaintance, operating in the San Francisco area, related that he had underestimated the investor interest. He forms land syndicates by gathering a group of prospective inactive investors together when he has a suitable property controlled. A fellow syndicator underwrites the deal by agreeing to take a number of limited partner interests if necessary to raise the needed funds.

In this instance the demand for participating limited partnership interests exceeded the supply needed to finance the equity in the syndicate, and some prospective investors were disappointed.

It pays to check and recheck carefully the estimates of capital which inactive investors might want to invest in a real estate syndicate.

Detail the syndicator's objectives

The syndicator, being the motivating force in the formation of the comtemplated real estate syndicate, includes in his setup those rewards for himself which appear to be fair and equitable.

When considering his objectives, the syndicator must give consideration to the requirement of governmental bodies which might have jurisdiction over his activities, because some states have what they call "standards of fair treatment" for the protection of investors. These "standards" limit the amount of profit which can be taken by the promoter as his share of the total profit.

The syndicator must also set up the deal so that it will attract investors, and this will require that their share of potential profits must be sufficient to get them to join in the venture.

The full disclosure of all details of a contemplated real estate syndicate in a sample format would include every amount to be paid to the syndicator, so the thing to do is to list the objectives, the rewards he expects to choose for his share. These could include the following:

1. Real estate commission (if the syndicator is in the real estate business).
2. Real estate management fees.
3. A profit to the syndicator for assignment of syndicator's contract to purchase real estate.
4. A share in the profits of operation (if income property).
5. A share in the capital gain.
6. A leaseback to syndicator of syndicate-owned real estate.

For instance, one syndicator stated that he operates only syndicates which purchase acreage, for capital gain. He gets control of the property by agreement to purchase, assigns his contract to purchase to a limited partnership syndicate in which he is the general partner and the other members are limited partners. They furnish all the capital and cover carrying charges, including a small management fee for him. When the property is resold, they get back their contributed capital, then the profits are divided, 50 per cent to him and 50 per cent to the limited partners in proportion to their contributions of capital.

This syndicator's objectives are *No. 2, Real estate management fee*, and *No. 5, A share in the capital gain.*

A syndicator must set up his goals in order to prepare a format for syndication. Choose yours from those listed or any others which seem to be fair and equitable.

Use a preliminary prospectus (see example in Chapter 8)

The preliminary prospectus, which is the format for the proposed real estate syndication, should include the following:

1. A descriptive statement, giving sufficient details about a property which would be suitable to syndicate. This can be a sample description, not a listing, but containing realistic figures showing that it would be a property which could be the basic real estate investment for a successful real estate syndication.
2. Contemplated distribution of "cash flow" to investors, computation of equity buildup and of depreciation to show "tax shelter."
3. A sample of the proposed syndicate agreement, showing full details of the intended operation, arrangements for management of the syndicate affairs and of the syndicate real estate, divisions of profits, and possibilities of future assessments against the investors.

Contact prospective investors

The preliminary prospectus, made up in several copies, furnishes all the ammunition needed to lay the groundwork for the formation of a real estate syndicate and to determine the feasibility of the project.

Tell the prospective investors how the proposed real estate syndicate would work out, and let them have a copy of the preliminary prospectus to study.

Starting out with a private syndicate, consisting of a relatively small group of investors, you will only need a few copies of the preliminary prospectus to hand out, and when they are returned they can be used again.

Contact the prospects by appointment, by casual meetings, or by assembling them. Some syndicators think that it helps to have a group together, so that they get the feeling that there are a number of people interested in such a venture, and that they are not being high-pressured into anything. Others feel that a luncheon meeting with one or two prospective investors is better, avoiding the mass approach, and lending dignity to the deal which then seems to be more personalized, inspiring confidence because of the more confidential approach.

Any way that the contact is made, the purpose of the meeting is educational, and meant to explain, by example, the working details of a real estate syndicate.

Make it crystal clear to the prospective investors that the sample prospectus features a parcel of real estate which would be suitable for syndication, but that the property is *not* the one which will be syndicated.

It is important to point out that no offering of securities of any kind is being made by this preliminary presentation. The format of a well-organized real estate syndicate is being exhibited by example, and that is all.

Naturally, any astute investor would be interested and perhaps excited by the potential profits which can be made by means of a real estate syndication.

A prospect cannot overlook the obvious advantages of pooling capital, expert handling of the project by a competent syndicator, ability to own a share in a property large enough to employ capable legal and tax counsel and to hire the maintenance of the property by experienced craftsmen.

The prospects should also be interested in knowing that they have no personal responsibilities in connection with such a venture, except to provide their share of the capital.

The generous returns which can be had from real estate which has been wisely chosen with skill, knowledge and experience should receive emphasis. Supporting this claim is the prospectus, featuring the property description which, as the example, will show what can be expected in the way of distributable "cash flow" far more than the return from any investment securities.

Attention should be directed to "tax shelter," the application of depreciation of improvements on real estate as a deduction from current, or ordinary, income. This item opens up a whole new field of thought to many prospective investors, and this income tax advantage is available only to owners of real estate. Investors who want to keep as much of their investment income as possible, by reducing their income taxes, cannot fail to be attracted by the "tax shelter" feature of syndicate-owned real estate. When and if the syndicate property is sold, the tax deferred by "tax shelter" is converted into favorably treated long-term gain for income tax purposes.

Potential capital gain should certainly be featured as an additional incentive to attract investors and to induce them to want to join in a real estate syndication. It is well known that prices of real estate increase because of the effects of inflation, scarcity, good management, and because of many other influences. Ownership of real estate is considered to be a fine hedge against inflation.

The focus of attention must be kept on the advantages of the syndication of real estate, however, and not on the ownership of real estate by the individual investor.

Make it known that a capable syndicator, by means of real estate syndication, overcomes the disadvantages of individual ownership of property.

The syndicator finds the right property for the syndicate to buy, at the best price possible, gets control of the property, handling all the complications of the deal, sets up the syndicate organization, and attracts investors to join the group. In addition to these important functions the syndicator manages the affairs of the syndicate and the syndicate real estate. When the time comes to sell the syndicate property the syndicator does the merchandising job to get the highest price obtainable in the prevailing market.

The format of the syndicate, the proper organization thereof, provides the framework which allows the syndicator to pass along to the investors the unique tax advantages of real estate, as well as limited liability and no management problems.

This is the picture which should be presented to the prospective syndicate investor when laying the groundwork.

The quality of the prospect list is going to be the determining factor as to the feasibility of the contemplated real estate syndication, provided that the groundwork is properly done.

Most syndicators are surprised to find the ready acceptance and eager interest with which their proposal is received. One syndicator stated that his visits to his doctor and dentist now center around a discussion of the profit opportunities of real estate, where in years past the subject of interest was golf or other sports. The real problem of these high-earning professional men is how to get involved in real estate ownership without all the complications and responsibilities of individual ownership. For them, joining in a real estate syndicate is the answer.

Laying the groundwork, that is, providing preliminary education about the workings of real estate syndication, when properly and thoroughly done, should convince the prospects of its merits. All of the problems of understanding the matter should have been thoroughly resolved.

Little more has to be done when prospective investors have been convinced of the merit of a project. Most well-screened prospects will ask to join the syndication when the time comes and it is ready for organization. Should they not volunteer to join the group, there should be only one question to ask when the syndicate is ready for organization, and that is, "Do you want a piece of this fantastic deal?"

Analyze prospect reaction

Using the card file of prospects, set down on each card impressions of their reaction to the proposal to form a real estate syndicate. Include every detail which the prospects have disclosed with regard to it, their expressions of interest, any preference for a different type of property for a syndication, and, if they do show interest, the amount of money they might invest.

When all cards are as completely detailed as possible, separate out the cards of the most logical prospects for a real estate syndicate of the type pictured in the sample prospectus.

A syndicator who wishes to take in active partners, fellow syndicators, will undoubtedly find them among those who have been sounded out while laying the groundwork. Those who have enough interest to want to be actively engaged in the syndication will usually let it be known. The syndicator should choose for a partner or partners, those who can be depended on to carry a part of the work involved, and to make such other contributions as may be needed by the syndicator. These contributions could be furnishing of capital for organization of the syndicate, and for an earnest money deposit on real estate to be purchased.

Analyzing the prospect cards is important. It might be found that there are prospects for more than one syndicate, or a larger project, or for several types of real estate. A syndicator is a specialist, but should be able to work with more than one type of property if there are those who can finance the equity.

Interested investors will tell of their interests and, if the syndication, as demonstrated in the sample prospectus, shows that a substantial profit could be made plus attractive tax advantages, then the prospects will be eager to participate in a real estate syndicate when the right property is found.

The total sum of the amounts which prospects will invest is the measure of the size of the syndication.

POINTS TO KEEP IN MIND

√ An individual with capital to invest wants complete information about an investment opportunity which is presented to him, and with which he is not entirely familiar.

√ An astute syndicator supplies the prospective investor with pertinent information regarding the operation of a real estate syndicate.

√ The information should include a sample prospectus based on a property of which the syndicator has knowledge.

√ The prospectus would show the complete format of a sample real estate syndicate, including the benefits which would accrue to a prospective investor and to the syndicator.

√ The information given and the sample prospectus are expected to line up the prospective investor as one of a group who will be eager to invest in a real estate syndicate when the syndicator controls suitable property.

√ The process of lining up a group of investors in order to form a real estate syndicate is called laying the groundwork.

CHAPTER 5—

Preliminary Organization

Organization should be handled in a methodical manner in order to achieve the desired setup with dispatch and to assure that the financial arrangements are to the satisfaction of the organizers.

The method of forming an organization is practically standardized, with steps in this order:

1. Planning.
2. Assembly of supporting data.
3. Missionary work.
4. Implementation (for preliminary organization).
5. Implementation (for permanent syndicate organization).

The formation of a preliminary organization is essential to formation of a real estate syndicate *only* if the original syndicator desires to take in one or more others as partners who will be fellow syndicators. The syndicator who forms a real estate syndicate by himself would follow much the same procedure, using the first three steps as outlined, setting up the details to suit himself, but would then proceed directly to the formation of the real estate syndicate. He would not need Step 4.

The purpose of taking in additional active partners as fellow syndicators is obvious. The original syndicator would consider taking others in on his deal only if these additional partners could make a valuable contribution to the venture, either by use of their judgment, skills, or knowledge of prospective inactive investors. These additional partners might also be expected to advance the money to pay for organizational expenses and to provide earnest money to tie up property which is to be syndicated.

Additional active partners will expect compensation for their part in activating the project. A definite arrangement will have to be made for an equitable division of the syndicator profits, if and when profits are made. Such an arrangement should be made in the form of a syndicators' agreement before inactive investors are brought into the group.

The preliminary organization can be formed by following these four steps:

PLANNING

For purposes of demonstration I make the following assumptions, concluding that the original syndicator's planning would have brought about these decisions and conditions:

- That one fellow syndicator is to be recruited.
- That the prospectus and format presented as examples in Chapter 8 will be used to substantiate the feasibility of the proposed real estate syndication, using the limited partnership form of organization.
- That a syndicators' agreement will be presented, somewhat similar in form to the example shown as Exhibit 5-1, in this chapter.
- That the prospective fellow syndicator has been briefed with information as detailed in Chapter 4, "Laying the Groundwork," and has shown interest in taking an active part in a real estate syndication.

The foregoing assumptions would really be decisions made by the original syndicator as a result of planning. Planning is, however, an integral part of all of the steps which are to be taken with relation to preliminary organization.

ASSEMBLY OF SUPPORTING DATA

Assembly of supporting data will have been well taken care of by the prior preparation of a preliminary prospectus similar to the one used as an example in Chapter 8.

It would be wise to use as the sample building one which exists, and about which knowledge is available. The price of the sample building should be in the range which is of interest for syndication, a price which would be one within the range of possibility for syndication with the capital which can be raised. Consideration should be given to the possible resale of the property when that appears to be advisable, and care should be taken to avoid acquiring a property which is too large to have a reasonable demand at that time. Prospective buyers for multimillion dollar properties are few, and because of this they are hard buyers, looking for bargains.

The data used for the purpose of recruiting additional syndicator partners would emphasize the profits to be made from the syndicators' activities.

In addition to the prospectus, the syndicator should provide a syndicators' agreement, possibly covering items as set forth in Exhibit 5-1. This sample syndicators' agreement is merely a guide to the syndicator and is by no means expected to be used without consulting competent legal counsel.

The points outlined in this sample agreement are some of the ones which must be well understood between syndicator partners, and this preliminary agreement might be drawn in such a way that it terminates upon formation of the syndicate organization, or it might continue as a separate agreement among the syndicators.

All details of a real estate syndication should be revealed to all parties concerned; the items in the syndicators' agreement which might affect the syndicate could be included in the syndicate agreement, so that there would be no possibility whatsoever of concealment.

EXHIBIT 5-1

A SAMPLE SYNDICATORS' AGREEMENT

AGREEMENT

THIS AGREEMENT, made this 1st day of December, A. D. 19__, at Chicago, Cook County, Illinois, between John J. Jones and Samuel S. Smith, both of the City of Chicago, County of Cook and State of Illinois, WITNESSETH:

The parties hereto make this agreement upon the following terms and conditions:

(a) That the parties hereto are desirous of forming a Real Estate Syndicate, the purpose of which is to deal in income-producing real estate, and the renting, operation and management of said real estate, in the State of Illinois, and,

(b) That the formation of said Real Estate Syndicate will require that a Limited Partnership be formed as the organizational vehicle for said Real Estate Syndicate, and,

(c) That the parties hereto intend to be the General Partners in said Limited Partnership, and,

(d) That certain organizational expenses will be incurred, and certain advances of capital be required, and,

(e) That Samuel S. Smith agrees to advance capital as required for the above purposes, in a sum not to exceed $10,000.00, and,

(f) That John J. Jones agrees that he is liable for one half of any sums advanced by said Samuel S. Smith, which liability will be evidenced and secured by notes the term of which shall not exceed one year from the date of said note, but with no interest to be paid by the borrower to the lender, and,

(g) That the parties hereto agree that they will not make any commitment for the expenditure of any monies so to be advanced, nor make any other commitment relating to the activities outlined in this Agreement without the consent of the other, and,

(f) That the parties hereto shall each own a one-half interest in the General Partner's share of the Limited Partnership, when, as, and if it is formed, and that they shall share equally in the profits or losses of said interest, and,

(g) That the Format for said Real Estate Syndication, a copy of which is attached hereto, and made a part hereof, shall be used, with such amendments as may be deemed advisable by legal counsel, but with division of profits, if any, and priority of payment of same to be made between the Limited Partners and General Partners as set forth in sample Limited Partnership Agreement which is a part of the prospectus which contains the Format for said real estate syndication, and,

(h) That, upon completion of the formation of the aforementioned Limited Partnership, and upon repayment of such sums of money as may have been advanced by Samuel S. Smith, as provided herein, which repayment is to be provided for in the Limited Partnership Agreement as proposed, thereupon, this Agreement shall be terminated, and become null and void, and the notes of John J. Jones, as given to Samuel S. Smith shall be canceled.

IN WITNESS WHEREOF, WE HAVE HEREUNTO SET OUR HANDS AND SEALS THE DAY AND YEAR ABOVE WRITTEN.

_____ (SEAL)   _____ (SEAL)

(This is a sample of a Syndicators' Agreement, only to be used as a guide to the items which might be covered in an agreement between syndicator partners in a preliminary organization.)

MISSIONARY WORK

"Missionary work," as applied to setting up of a preliminary organization, will probably have been partly done while laying the groundwork. The partner or partners to be taken in as fellow syndicators to join in the activation of the real estate syndicate are often found among the prospective inactive investors. Their interest, whetted by familiarizing them with the working details of a real estate syndicate, motivates some prospects to want to take an active part in the deal.

These parties express interest in the active end of the job, and it is up to the syndicator to evaluate their qualifications to determine what constructive help they can give him before inviting any of them into partnership as fellow syndicators.

While laying the groundwork, the original syndicator has been telling prospective investors of his intention to form a syndicate to operate with real estate, and how it works, but he has, at the same time, been accumulating information about the prospects. Therefore, both the original syndicator and the party who is interested in becoming his partner, already are grounded with information which may be enough to be a basis for agreement.

Some syndicators, when first thinking about organizing a real estate syndicate, have in mind people who would be desirable as fellow syndicators, and these would be approached early, to be a part of the setup when the formation of the real estate syndicate becomes a prime objective.

The additional syndicator partners might be in the legal or accounting professions, or could be able to furnish capital and contribute other valuable services.

"Missionary work" continues into the preliminary organizational meeting. Note that the first three items on the agenda of that meeting, a sample of which is shown as Exhibit 5-2, are concerned with a review of syndicate operation and with discussions which lead to a meeting of the minds of the parties prior to "implementation," the formation of the preliminary organization.

IMPLEMENTATION (OF PRELIMINARY ORGANIZATION)

The original syndicator, prepared with data which support the formation of a real estate syndication, and which show the feasibility of such an activity, now sets up a meeting with his prospective fellow syndicator to wrap up the formation of a preliminary organization.

Our assumption was that only one fellow syndicator was to be recruited, so that this meeting can be an informal one, a luncheon, or just an appointment meeting, but with enough time assigned to the meeting so that all details can be thoroughly discussed, and the preliminary organization formed.

An agenda is necessary for this meeting, and it should be prepared by the original syndicator to keep procedures moving in an orderly manner, and to present the subject matter with the original syndicator's objectives fully in mind. Exhibit 5-2 is a sample agenda. Other items may be added if appropriate.

EXHIBIT 5-2

AGENDA

1. Review of prospectus.

2. Presentation of syndicators' agreement.

3. Discussion of proposed duties to be assigned to each syndicator.

4. Signing of preliminary agreement to organize a real estate syndicate.

5. Selection of an attorney to act as legal counsel.

6. Arrangements for handling funds for preliminary organization.

7. Discussion of methods of obtaining listings of property to be considered for syndication, and methods of keeping records of same.

8. Discussion of additional efforts toward laying the groundwork.

9. Arrangements for future meetings.

10. Other business.

Note : Several copies of the agenda should be prepared so that copies can be used as worksheets and to keep for reference. Room should be left for additional subjects.

Item 1 on the agenda is self-explanatory. *The review of the sample brochure* is to make sure that the prospective syndicator understands the setup thoroughly.

Item 2—Presentation of the syndicators' agreement requires some thought. The original syndicator will have included in this agreement the division of the syndicators' profits which is proposed by him, and the delegation of duties. The original syndicator should decide if these subjects are open to negotiation. Should he decide that these subjects are not subject to change, then the prospective partner can only accept the deal or decline to join in the venture.

Item 3, A discussion of the proposed duties to be assigned to each syndicator: A decision must be made when the agenda is prepared if this item is to be open to discussion, or if it is to be a condition which is to be determined by the original syndicator.

Up to this point every move made by the original syndicator in guiding the meeting has been directed toward reaching the point of decision, the actual setting up of the preliminary organization, the goal of which is to form a real estate syndicate.

Discussion of points vital to a meeting of the minds of those at this meeting should have been disposed of by now. Only implementation remains to be accomplished.

*Item 4—Signing the preliminary agreement to organize a real estate syndicate—*This is the start of implementation. When the agreement is signed, action can begin. If the deal is a good one, the prospective syndicator partner will be eager to sign the agreement and to get going. If this is not the case, and the deal is a good one, then the original syndicator should look for another partner.

When the syndicators' agreement has been executed, it is in order to proceed to the next items on the agenda, which are to be discussed by the syndicators as partners, and acted upon.

Item 5—Selection of an attorney. The selection of the proper attorney to guide the partners is most important and should receive careful consideration. A competent, knowledgeable attorney can provide the syndicators and the real estate syndicate with invaluable service.

Advice on employment of professional services is amplified in Chapter 6, but some coverage is necessary at this point to stress the urgency of obtaining good legal counsel at the beginning of organization.

The attorney chosen should be familiar with the formation of the type of organization which fits the operation best and which is to be used as the framework of the real estate syndication. He should be alert to the wording and proper construction of the syndicate agreement which makes it possible to minimize taxes on income of the group and the individual members thereof.

An attorney should not be chosen or employed just because he is a friend, but because his knowledge and ability are such that he can make a valuable contribution to the venture, at a price which is relevant to the value of his services.

The matter of selection and employment of an attorney should be promptly attended to, so that the organization of the syndicate proceeds within the framework of laws of all governmental bodies having jurisdiction.

This attorney should review the partners' preliminary agreement and make recommendations for appropriate amendments or additions if needed. He should also review the preliminary prospectus and make needed changes. He should make sure that the syndicators have a well-drawn syndicate agreement ready for inspection by investors, and he should be able to activate the real estate syndicate without delay when property is controlled and inactive investors ready to contribute capital to the venture.

Item 6—Arrangements for handling funds for preliminary organization. This is simply the matter of providing a bank account for the purpose of paying for the preliminary organizational expenses, and the depositing of funds for this purpose. The earnest money deposit which later will be made when contracting to purchase real estate should also be handled through this account, so that it is well established that the syndicators control the property which is to be syndicated, by means of this contract and deposit of money.

Some simple name should be worked out, on advice of counsel, for the preliminary organization and for the bank account. This could be just the names of the syndicators.

*Item 7—Methods of listing—*see Chapter 10.

*Item 8—Additional efforts on laying the Groundwork—*see Chapter 4. The new partner undoubtedly has contacts with people who would be prospective inactive investors in a real estate syndicate. He should be briefed on laying the groundwork. The new partner then might be able to easily double the number of investor prospects, making it possible to purchase a larger property, or to form more than one real estate syndicate.

Item 9—Arrangements for future meetings. No explanation is needed. Further meetings of the syndicators are required and should be arranged for. A minute book should be kept, so that decisions, once made, will be recorded for future reference.

KEEP THESE POINTS IN MIND

√ A preliminary organization is only necessary if a syndicator desires to take in one or more syndicator partners.

√ Should the syndicator desire to take in one or more syndicator partners, then a meeting should be arranged with the prospective syndicator partners.

√ The original syndicator should thoroughly organize the meeting with a carefully drawn agenda and agreement documents to formalize the deal.

√ The original syndicator should determine in advance which items of agreement with additional syndicator partners will be negotiable.

√ Note should be made of points of agreement with regard to items in the agenda.

√ Wrap up the meeting by executing agreements as worked out.

CHAPTER 6—

Employment of Services

A real estate syndicate can, by reason of pooling of the capital of the group of investors, purchase a major property. The syndicator therefore can afford to employ expert professional counsel and service, and should do so from the inception of the deal.

These are the professionals who should be employed in order to produce the best results from a real estate syndicate:

- The attorney
- The accountant
- The real estate broker
- The real estate manager
- The mortgage broker

Each of these professionals has a valuable contribution to make to a syndicator and to the real estate syndicate, from the beginning of the formation of the syndicate to its conclusion. The part that each shall play in the activity should be well thought out, their individual competence thoroughly checked out, the cost of their services considered and, if possible, determined in advance.

A knowledgeable syndicator knows what services are needed from each of these professionals, and makes an efficient use of their services without allowing the cost of it to become a burden which would unduly reduce the profit potential of the real estate syndication.

The selection of these important professional people, by careful consideration of their qualifications and negotiation for their services, assures the syndicator of the competent counsel and service which is required, at a cost which is reasonable, and predictable.

The method of selection of each can be divided into two parts, the first being the generalized qualifications which could apply to all of the professionals, and the second being an outline of the scope of the work required to be performed by each, and the items subject to negotiation as to their charges, in order to have a full understanding before employing them.

The generalized qualifications could be described in this way:

The employment of the professionals needed by the syndicator should be based on the professional's ability to measure up reasonably to the following standards.

That the party to be employed:

1. Is competent to do the required job, is experienced and easy to work with.
2. Is efficient and able to turn out the assigned work rapidly to minimize charges, and to do the job promptly to prevent delays which might cause problems for the syndicator.
3. Is able to quote an hourly rate for this time (applies only to attorney and accountant). He should also be able to quote outside prices to cover certain phases of the job to be done, including charges for permits. The charges, when made for work completed, should be based on the hourly rate or the outside price for the job, whichever is least.

The real estate broker, real estate manager, and mortgage broker should be able to make solid commitments as to fees, commissions and other charges which might be a part of organizing the syndicate, finding the investment, managing or financing the real estate of the syndicate.

All quotations of fees, costs or charges should be made in writing when a deal is made to employ the services of these professionals, and in advance of the employment if possible. There should be a specific recitation of the work to be done, permit or other charges to be included, and the time for completion of the work, if that applies.

When the syndicator is satisfied that these generalized qualifications have been met, then a more detailed discussion of the scope of the work of each professional can be arranged by the syndicator to finalize the terms on which employment will be based.

The scope of the work of each of the professionals to be employed could be along the lines detailed hereafter.

THE ATTORNEY

The scope of the work which would be needed to be done by an attorney, for the syndicator in the formation of the real estate syndicate and for the syndicator and the real estate syndicate after it is in operation, would include:

1. Review the syndicators' agreement, if there is one. Suggest revisions or amendments to agreement if indicated.
2. Review sample prospectus to check legal details and suggest changes he thinks necessary.

3. Give opinion regarding "private syndicate" status.

4. Determine, by consultation with syndicator, the type of organization which is to be the vehicle of the syndication.

5. Prepare a facsimile of the organizational agreement for use in the sample prospectus. This form should be drawn in such a complete manner that with small insertions it could be used to activate a real estate syndicate without delay when the time is right. In the event that the organizational vehicle is to be a limited partnership, the facsimile would be a form for limited partnership, an agreement which could be utilized by filling in pertinent details when the syndicator has a property controlled, and is ready to activate the syndicate organization.

6. Review all transactions of the syndicator which involve the syndicate to a significant extent, including any contract to purchase or sell real estate, financing the real estate, leasing for a term of years, building or remodeling contracts, and any other contracts which the syndicator might enter into on behalf of the real estate syndicate.

The attorney who is being considered should be willing to quote an hourly charge for legal work as outlined, and to quote an outside package price for doing various phases of the work, including filing fees, or any other costs. The syndicator should arrange that, if employed, the attorney will undertake to do work as specified, and to take the hourly rate in payment if that is less than the bid figure for work performed. It would be advisable to get a package figure to do all of the legal work to carry the syndication to the point where it is an operating organization, which would be when the property to be acquired is owned and being operated by the syndicate.

The syndicator should get a letter from the attorney who is being considered, covering work to be done and the charges to be made for it. Any other legal work necessary because of local conditions should be included in the proposal. Such a commitment from an attorney enables the syndicator to estimate the cost of organizing the real estate syndicate.

Preliminary legal work, consisting of a review of the syndicator agreement and of the sample prospectus, an opinion as to the "private syndicate" status, and preparation of facsimile syndicate agreement prospectus—these items, constituting the first phase of legal work needed to lay the groundwork, require immediate attention when a syndicate is being contemplated. The attorney who is selected should be authorized to do this work as soon as possible while the deal is being worked out, and this work should be paid for upon completion.

Recently, when our small syndicate was about to develop a residential cooperative which we estimated would be in the million-dollar class, we were unable to find a local attorney with experience enough for our purpose. Those attorneys we did contact offered to research the matter, and thought that they could then handle the job. We therefore employed the senior partner in a large law firm in the Los Angeles area, who had successfully handled the legal work for many cooperative developments. He committed himself to outside prices for the various phases of the work, and did an eminently satisfactory job. Now there are several local attorneys who are well versed in the procedures for organization of condominium and cooperative developments.

I would avoid any deal which would give an attorney, or any other professional, a share in the project for his services. The temptation is to give too great a share for the services. Most professional men are very astute, and would not give their services unless they thought that they had a pretty sure thing going, and if this is the case, then they should get paid a fair price for their work, and get paid in cash. Should they wish to join the syndicate group, the joining should be a separate transaction.

To sum up—seek out an attorney who is qualified, give him a full picture of your aims and requirements with reference to his legal work, get a price for the work which can be depended on for estimating organizational costs, be sure that the quoted price will be good when the services are needed, then hold the quotation until ready to proceed with the matter. Preliminary organizational legal work should always be separately priced.

THE ACCOUNTANT

Accurate records are essential to the operation of a real estate syndicate. The employment of a capable and respected accountant early in the organization of a real estate syndicate is mandatory.

Working with the attorney, the accountant provides tax counsel, and the original setup of records is the basis for substantial tax savings, when the job is properly done.

Scope of the accountant's work

At the beginning of the organization of the real estate syndicate, a set of accounting books and records must be provided. Methods of application of depreciation of improvements on real estate for income tax purposes must be decided. After being approved by the attorney, all prospectuses, agreements and other pertinent documents should be submitted to the accountant chosen, for his review and to enable him to set up the records properly. When the deal closes for the acquisition of the property by the real estate syndicate, the closing statement showing the full details of the purchase transaction must be incorporated in the records of the organization.

All of the foregoing items are a part of preliminary organization to such a degree that a quotation for this portion of the work should be obtained. This part of the accountant's job is a one-time operation, and should include the supplies of record books needed to get the accounting operational.

The accounting operation might include the receiving of rents from tenants occupying the syndicate property, and the payment of current bills when due. In such a case, the management work is being divided, since someone else usually undertakes to do the negotiating with tenants and handles the other duties which a real estate manager covers. A monthly fee should be negotiated for this phase of the operational work with the accountant, if he is to do this job.

My experience has been, as one of the syndicators, that the responsibility for management was ours, and the accountant took our monthly rent statements into his records to record completely the operations of the syndicate. The accountant closed the syndicate books annually, made out all tax reports, and furnished the syndicate members with copies, together with an annual statement of operations of the syndicate. This climaxed and supported the monthly rent statements showing operations of the property which we, as the real estate managers, sent to all members of the group who made up the syndicate. Obviously this method of operating syndicate property reduced the charges for accounting to a minimum, but we obtained figures estimating the costs of the accounting to be done, with maximums as outside prices where we could do so.

With regard to the employment of an accountant, the procedure which the syndicator adopts is to determine that he is qualified, present him with the accounting picture, get quotations for preliminary work to be done, and for recurring accounting work, fit these figures into the computation of organizational costs and operating estimates, and make a written agreement with him when ready to activate the real estate syndicate.

THE REAL ESTATE BROKER

One of the syndicators might be a real estate broker, and still furnish professional services which could cost the real estate syndicate money. Any charges to be made to the syndicate by a broker, or any commissions which the broker might make by reason of dealing with the real estate syndicate as the purchaser of property, should be fully understood in advance and disclosed in full.

A real estate broker who is not a member of the syndicate, and is not the syndicator, when employed as the exclusive agent for the group in buying or selling property for the syndicate, should be expected to meet the basic standards of professionals to be employed, and also:

1. Diligently seek out listings of property of the type and size which meets the requirements of the syndicate, and in the locale as designated.
2. Furnish complete details about said property, as fully set out in Chapter 10, "Finding the Investment."
3. Cooperate with any and all other brokers who might have property listed which could interest his principal, the real estate syndicate.
4. Negotiate on behalf of his buyer for the purchase of the property.
5. Receive his compensation, (commission on the sale when and if made to his principal) from the seller of the property.

When syndicate property is to be sold he should:

1. Vigorously promote the sale of the property of the syndicate, at a price which has been set by, and is acceptable to the seller, the syndicate.
2. Advertise the property in an effective way.
3. Prepare material for advertising, and a brochure for use in promoting the property sale.
4. Cooperate with other brokers in every way possible to effect a sale of the property.
5. Receive his compensation (real estate sale commission) from the seller, the syndicate.

In short, a competent syndicator, representing his syndicate in dealing with a real estate broker who is not a member of the real estate syndicate, should have all of the details of the employment of the broker clearly understood and in writing, if the broker is to be given any exclusive rights to represent the syndicate.

The agreement should clearly cover all details of the employment, including the duties of the broker, what representations he is authorized to make as agent for the syndicate, the term of his employment, the compensation he is to get, when it is "earned," and who is to pay it.

It is not enough to state that the compensation will be the "usual" real estate commission. It is not unusual to base the compensation of the broker on the recommended rate of commission of a local real estate board, but there is no substitute for being specific. State that the broker's commission shall be a certain percentage of the gross sales price, or whatever other specific agreement is made, and when the sale contract is drawn, insert the amount of cash to be paid to the broker when the deal is consummated.

When the real estate broker is also the syndicator, he sets up his deal in the preliminary syndicate agreement, and in the prospectus, as well as inserting full details in the syndicate organizational agreement, so that there can be no misunderstanding on the part of anyone with reference to his employment.

There are syndicators who are not brokers who do not employ any broker as their exclusive representative, but deal directly with owners and with any broker who might present an interesting deal. It appears that an owner—syndicate, corporation or other— can deal with its own property without a real estate license but, of course, cannot collect real estate commissions.

THE REAL ESTATE MANAGER

Provided that a real estate manager is found who meets the applicable general standards, the scope of his work and negotiations for his employment could be like this:

The scope of the real estate manager's work

A property manager should take over all of the burdens of management of real estate, including leasing, rent collection, payment of bills out of rents collected, letting contracts for maintenance, rendering monthly statements of operations, from which he deducts his management fees. The net monthly rental is disposed of as directed by the owner, which in this case would be the syndicator, acting for the syndicate which owns the property.

It is usual to impose a limitation of the amount of money which can be spent by the managing agent as set forth in the contract. Most management firms do not furnish a bond, probably because they turn over the net rents every month to the owner of the property, and thus do not carry large balances of the owner's cash on hand.

Negotiating the management contract

The details of a real estate management contract should be thoroughly and carefully worked out prior to engaging an agent.

Management of real estate in various parts of the nation is not a uniform service, and for this reason it would be wise to obtain copies of sample real estate management contracts from several real estate managers in the locale where operations are to be conducted.

Comparison of the methods and arrangements customary in the area and the rates asked for services to be rendered easily resolves the problems of employing a manager for syndicate property. One point should be emphasized, and that is that the contract should contain a definite arrangement with regard to the right of the owner to terminate the management contract by giving agreed notice, and the contract should terminate if the property is sold.

A syndicator who expects to manage syndicate property personally would do well to obtain copies of real estate management contracts in the area of operations, to support his proposed management fees, and to determine the scope of the work to be done for this fee. The duties of the syndicator manager should be as well defined as would be the case if a management firm did the job.

The problem of employing a real estate manager can be solved by checking his qualifications, determining the work which is to be done by the manager, getting a quotation of the cost of doing the work, and using this cost in the operational expense of property which might be acquired by the syndicate. Activating the employment can be quickly done by executing a management contract when the property is bought.

THE MORTGAGE BROKER

The mortgage business is highly competitive, and the lenders and their agents are constantly striving for the highest returns on the loans they make, utmost security and biggest charges for making the loan.

This leads them to emphasize the attractions of the loan which they might consider making, and to gloss over the details which might be considered unpleasant by the borrower.

An astute borrower is naturally interested in obtaining a loan which suits his purpose, and this might be to get a conservative 60 per cent loan, or an extremely "leveraged" loan. In either case, the borrower usually wants to get the lowest interest rate possible, the longest term of loan, the lowest loan fee, or charges, and to avoid personal liability for the loan.

The aims of the lender and the borrower are the usual ones, supporting the competitive American system of negotiation by adversaries to work out a "meeting of the minds," so that a business deal can be made between the parties.

The loan application, which is the document which supposedly details the requirements of the borrower with reference to making the loan, often touches only on these few points. In the event that the lender "accepts" the loan application of the prospective borrower, the documents which constitute the mortgage, the note, the mortgage or trust deed, and other forceful legal instruments, are presented for the signature of the borrower. The loan documents could contain provisions which would be unacceptable if explained to the borrower, and if there was time to get another loan.

These are some of the items which should be settled *before* a loan application is signed. Most of them should be covered in the loan application.

1. Is the mortgage broker a direct lender's representative, or an independent broker, using the loan application and deposit to tie up the borrower while "hawking" the loan around among prospective lenders?

2. Can the lender's agent or representative give positive assurance that the lender will make a loan in the area of interest?

3. Will samples of the loan application and all other loan documents be furnished in advance of making the loan application for study by the borrower and his legal adviser?

4. What will be the cost of making the loan, if any? This sometimes is designated as a "loan fee" or "points."

5. What deposit will be required with the loan application, if any? Will this deposit be placed in escrow? Will the deposit be applied against the "loan fee" if the loan is accepted? Will the deposit be forfeited by the borrower if the loan is accepted and the borrower does not go through with the deal? Will the deposit be promptly returned if the loan is not accepted within the time designated?

6. How much time is to be allowed for the lender to accept the loan application?

7. Will there be penalties which the borrower must pay for full prepayment of the loan before maturity? For partial prepayment? What portion of the principal of the loan will be paid off when partial prepayments of principal are made by the borrower? (When refinancing, these items should be carefully checked in the loan then on the property, to make sure that refinancing is possible, or economically feasible.)

8. Will there be a charge for a loan appraisal?

9. Will there be penalties for late payment of installments of interest and principal?

10. What insurance will be required? Who can write this?

11. What assurance can be given as to availability of mortgage funds when borrower needs the money?

12. Will there be any restrictions on secondary financing of the property by borrower?

13. What guarantees will be required of borrower, and what liability will be incurred by the borrower?

14. Will an assignment of rents be required to secure payments by borrower when due?

15. Are there any restrictions on occupancy of property?

16. Will there be an escalation clause, allowing the lender to require that the loan be paid off in full if the property is sold?

17. Could a subsequent owner buy the property subject to the loan, or would such buyer be required to assume it?

18. Will a land survey be required?

19. What type mortgage title policy is required, and at what cost?

20. Will a mortgage escrow be required? Who pays? How much?

A mortgage broker becomes employed when a borrower signs an application for a real estate loan, but the prospective borrower then becomes tied up and cannot freely shop around for a loan with other lending agencies.

This is an important statement, because too many prospective borrowers think that a loan application is just an inquiry to be made in order to determine what kind of loan can be made on a parcel of real estate.

My experience has been that loan documents almost always contain provisions which a borrower would not accept if they were pointed out, and if the consequences of their imposition were fully known. The time to eliminate many of the objectionable items is before the loan application is signed.

I suggest that, when negotiating a real estate loan, a syndicator who desires a loan should secure a firm loan commitment in advance of signing any document whatsoever, if that is possible. Further, that sample copies of all documents be furnished for study, and for review by legal counsel for the borrower. The commitment should state that there will be no charges of any kind to be made in connection with making the mortgage loan which are not included in the commitment letter.

The commitment should be good for a specified time, long enough so that a syndicate could be organized to make use of the loan proposed.

The liabilities of those who sign the loan documents should be determined, and requirements for guarantors resolved.

The device of organizing a corporation for the express purpose of executing loan documents to avoid personal liability is an expensive and useless procedure if the lending source also demands personal guarantees.

One attorney who syndicates real estate stated that he opens negotiations with lending agencies by bluntly rejecting any thought of personal liabilities or guarantees. He insists that the loan commitment or application should provide for the waiver of personal liability if the loan is made.

Mortgage lenders can be extremely helpful and important to a syndicator, by way of providing "leverage" which produces the high net income that attracts investors. Use their services with knowledge and caution.

POINTS TO KEEP IN MIND

√ A syndicator should employ the services of competent professionals when forming a real estate syndicate.

√ A wise syndicator carefully considers the advice of the professionals employed before making decisions or taking any action towards the formation of a real estate syndicate.

√ The scope of the work of each of the professionals to be employed should be carefully worked out, so that the syndicator and the party employed understand each other.

√ The charges to be made by the professional to be employed should be quoted in writing, preferably for a package deal.

√ The estimated cost of professional assistance to the syndicator is to be included in the estimated cost of organizing the real estate syndicate.

CHAPTER 7—

Finding and Attracting

Investors

Finding investors for a real estate syndicate can be done by recruiting one's friends, relatives and acquaintances to form a so called "private" syndicate, or it can be done in some states by means of advertising and using the services of real estate brokers and syndicate brokers to form a "public" syndicate.

For purposes of this *Manual and Guide*, I will assume that a syndicator starting out would want to organize a *private real estate syndicate*. The public real estate syndicate will be described fully enough in Chapter 9 so that a new syndicator will clearly recognize the difference between the two types. Experience with a *private syndicate* may lead to a progression to the more complicated and sophisticated *public real estate syndicate*, provided that such activity is permitted in the state in which the syndicator wishes to operate.

Finding and attracting investors for a private real estate syndicate is a public relations job, and an extension of the procedures outlined in Chapter 4, "Laying the Groundwork."

Finding and Attracting Investors for a private syndicate can be done this way:

- Select the best prospects from the list of prospective investors made while laying the groundwork.
- Keep contact with the prospects who have expressed interest.
- Check to make sure that the prospects understand the prospectus.
- Probe for the amounts that the prospects could invest.
- Ask prospective investors for leads to other prospects.
- Watch the newspapers and other publications.
- Keep a scrapbook.

- Keep prospects informed.
- Dangle the bait of bigger profits from real estate syndication.

Finding and attracting investors is a methodical job of public relations, so it is worth while to detail further these nine procedures to add emphasis to each.

SELECT THE BEST PROSPECTS

Selecting the best prospects is really a weeding-out process, and frequent contact with the prospects on the list makes the selection almost automatic. Some of the prospective investors will just flatly say that they are uninterested, or may be uninterested at that time. Others may say that they are ready to go ahead when the syndicate is ready for activation.

The card file system of keeping track of prospects permits the filing away of those who are not presently interested, and narrows the field to those who show real interest.

I suggest that no prospect cards be destroyed. A prospect may suddenly inherit money, or sell other investments, and become a live, eager investor overnight.

A syndicator who watches the news items, the real estate transfers, obituaries and legal notices, can find many names of parties who could participate in a real estate syndicate.

CONTACTING PROSPECTIVE INVESTORS

There are innumerable methods for making and keeping contact with prospective investors. Each syndicator should choose the method which suits him and the situation.

The syndicator of a "private syndicate" would be acquainted with his prospective investors.

The initial approach to these prospects to make the original contact for the purpose of promoting the formation of a real estate syndicate could be direct and informal. The syndicator simply calls the prospect on the telephone and states that he is planning on organizing a real estate syndicate. He then goes on to say that he would like to call on the prospect to explain the workings of a real estate syndicate, the profits to be made and the tax advantages to be gained. The syndicator makes it known that he will show the prospect a sample of the format for a real estate syndicate of the type he visualizes. He suggests that the prospect would certainly want to know about this profitable form of investment, and to participate when the syndicator controls a suitable property.

Some syndicators arrange a meeting of prospective investors to explain the advantages of investing in a real estate syndicate. At a later meeting the Syndicator gathers the most interested prospective investors to tell them of the property he now controls, and to sell them on the idea of setting up the organization on that occasion.

Recently, I was told by a local syndicator that over $400,000 was raised at such a meeting for the formation of a real estate syndicate to develop a convalescent hospital, in which the units of participation were a minimum of $12,500.

Some such approach must be used in some states in order to retain the status of a "private syndicate" which avoids complexities of obtaining permits from the state governing bodies.

A syndicator who is organizing a "public syndicate" could advertise and approach prospective investors by direct mail, but he would be required to get a permit from the Corporation Commissioner in some states. The Corporation Commissioner of the State of California, for example, takes the position that no permit should be issued for "public offering" of participating interests in limited partnerships.

In California, therefore, a syndicator who wants to solicit prospective investors who are not personally known to him, must use a more sophisticated business organization such as a corporation to be the vehicle for his real estate syndicate. He then faces the expenses of forming such an organization, and forfeits the favorable income tax position of the limited partnership.

The heavy burden of corporate taxes, and the fact that depreciation is locked into the corporation, makes a public syndicate much less attractive to both syndicator and to the prospective investor.

Contacts with prospective real estate syndicate investors can be kept alive when lunching at the same restaurant, at the golf club, family gatherings, card games, and by purposeful business calls. I have found that delegates to volunteer political organization conventions, gathered from the entire State of California, with diversified business interests, form a cross-section of people with a remarkable interest in the subject of real estate syndication. Several of these have later inquired about joining in a syndication.

A Chicago syndicator of my acquaintance, an attorney, learned to trap shoot so that he could go duck hunting with wealthy men who could be induced to join his real estate syndicates. This syndicator operated with almost no supporting data and no prospectus. He just kept contact with his wealthy duckhunter prospects. He kept dropping remarks about the real estate bargains he could buy if he only had the money available.

"If I had ten men with $50,000 each, or five men to invest $100,000 each," he would say to them, "I could double their money and make a 10 per cent return for them while holding the property." He whetted their appetites for big profits.

There were many other syndicators operating in the Chicago area at the time, but most were handling capital gain deals. This person was syndicating for income, and with the intention of keeping and managing the properties for rent profits. Not a new idea, of course, but one which was then just gaining favor again. The era of real estate bond issue "leverage" had ended, and he was getting his "leverage" by means of syndicating the building equities.

This Chicago lawyer syndicated several million dollars' worth of properties. He employed a number of his relatives in the management of the property, which included two large motion picture theaters, and a number of office, commercial and hotel buildings. His friends estimated that he made more than $1 million for himself, and big profits for his syndicate investors. His approach to his prospects was simple and always the same— "I could double the money of five or ten men with $10,000 each, and produce a good income while doing it." "Let me buy real estate with your money, and I will manage it to make big profits for you."

This lawyer and other syndicators put millions of dollars worth of real estate syndicates together, mostly organized among business acquaintances.

Each syndicator must figure out his own way to keep contact with his prospective real estate syndicate investors, so that they are fully informed and ready to join his real estate syndicate when the right property is controlled.

MAKE SURE THAT THE PROSPECTS UNDERSTAND THE PROSPECTUS

Most people do not understand the workings of a real estate syndicate, even though they were indoctrinated by the syndicator when he was laying the groundwork. Showing the prospects a sample prospectus helps considerably, but it takes several contacts to point out the big profit potential and the unique tax advantages which can be had by joining in a real estate syndication. When the subject of real estate syndication is fully understood by prospective investors, then they become excited enough to offer to join one, and to look forward to substantial rewards.

News items which appear in the press are frequently used to demonstrate what can be done by means of real estate syndication, or are used by a syndicator to open up the field of questions which are unresolved in the mind of the prospective investor.

When the prospective investor realizes that the syndicator is presenting a fine opportunity to make money in a type of real estate investment which the prospect could not handle by himself, and that he has little personal liability and no management problems, then the prospect is ready for the venture.

PROBE FOR AMOUNTS PROSPECTS CAN INVEST

People who have cash on hand to invest are reluctant to disclose the amount they have available. This is a natural precaution, one which a syndicator must overcome by gaining the confidence of the prospective real estate syndicate investor.

Gaining the confidence of people who have money to invest is a matter of getting better acquainted by means of frequent contacts with them and associating with other people who command the respect of the prospects, such as friends, relatives or mutual business acquaintances. Naming these people helps establish the background of capability, reputation and integrity of the syndicator.

A salesman for a mutual fund investment company recently called on me to sell shares in the company he represented. He had phoned for the appointment, stating that one of his customers, a mutual acquaintance, had given him my name. He stated that my friend had been so pleased with the high returns from the stock which he had purchased that by giving the salesman my name he was doing me a favor.

This salesman was well supplied with data which supported his claims for potential capital gains and high income. This could be had by purchasing his mutual funds stock. He named several other acquaintances and told how much they had invested through him. He probed repeatedly to determine how much I had to invest, and what it was invested in. There was a deal, he said, whereby a lesser commission would be charged if $25,000 were to be invested. When I did not respond to this, I was told that this deal could be made if $25,000 was invested over a period of one year. He was a good salesman, but I did not buy from him, since my interests are in real estate investments.

The mutual stock salesman was not easily discouraged, however. He kept dropping in every few days, and on one visit he sold $10,000 worth of stock to another man in the office. He was a salesman! He probed and succeeded.

A syndicator has a much easier time selling interests in a real estate syndicate, and in probing for the amounts which the prospect could invest in a real estate syndicate.

First of all, the syndicator who is organizing a private syndicate is contacting friends, relatives, and acquaintances.

Second, the deal presented offers high returns and a good chance of capital gains, with no more liability than ownership of stock. There are no management problems.

Third, there are unique tax advantages to participation in a real estate syndicate.

The presentation of these unusual investment advantages, supported by a prospectus which gives examples of what can be done by syndication, gives the syndicator chances to probe for the amounts which his prospective investor might be able to contribute as a participant in such a venture.

A syndicator can afford to use the "soft sell" methods on his prospects because the profits to be made in the field of real estate so far outstrip the returns possible from other investments. The "soft sell" means that the syndicator is not selling the deal which he is exhibiting as an example, but that he will have such a deal soon.

Implant in the mind of the prospective investor that, when a deal is ready, he might be invited to join in and make the big profits. Get him so sold he asks to join in.

Probe for the amount that a prospective investor can contribute as a member of a real estate syndicate.

ASK THE PROSPECTIVE INVESTOR FOR LEADS

Asking prospective investors for leads is only good business. This is a first-class way to expand the list of prospective investors. The lead may be even a better prospect than the one who gives the name, since conversations between them may have revealed a keen interest in real estate as an investment, often by one who does not have enough cash to buy a major property by himself.

Give special attention to leads on prospective investors who can benefit the most from joining a real estate syndicate. High-income professionals, doctors, dentists, scientists, lawyers, entertainment figures and highly paid executives are examples. Their energies are directed to their regular occupation, and they often put their savings into low-return securities because they simply do not have time for real estate which they own themselves. Syndicate ownership is the solution for them, if they only get to know about how it works.

WATCH THE NEWSPAPERS

An alert syndicator watches the newspapers and other news media, financial publications and builders' news.

It is interesting to see the number of items which pertain to real estate syndication, and fascinating to trace the methods used by syndicators to work out their deals. One such item, which I saw in a large metropolitan newspaper, reported that a group of teachers had formed an investment group which, while it was a credit union, did handle some direct real estate operations by means of forming limited partnerships consisting of members of the credit union.

A statement by the director of this credit union was reported as follows: "By pooling teacher talents and resources, limited income teachers will be able to individually invest relatively small amounts of financing to collectively obtain advantages available in major real estate transactions." He went on to say, "For example, under limited partnership arrangements among participating members, and with financial assistance of a major savings and loan association, $100,000 has been invested in property in Hollywood, and $240,000 on an improved property purchase of multiple units in Beverly Hills."

This syndicator was *finding and attracting investors* from his own built-in group of prospects, and he did not have to probe for how much they could invest.

The credit union makes real estate loans, so that the director has a workable knowledge of real estate and values. The method used by these teachers is different, since the syndicate groups are recruited out of a savings group, but it is a good deal for them, because they can save until they have enough to participate in the higher earnings and unique tax advantages of real estate ownership, with expert management, and joined with a group of friends.

There are frequent news items concerning the transactions of real estate syndicates, giving the names of the members of the syndicate and the type of property which is the investment. The names of the syndicate members should be listed as future prospective investors.

KEEP A SCRAPBOOK

Clip out news items which report transactions of real estate syndicates, and other items in the news media which support investment in real estate, and especially where there is a clear indication that a profit has been made.

Keep a scrapbook of these items, and of all items which indicate that special influences are forcing prices of real estate up in your area of interest for syndication.

For instance, I point out that Oxnard and Port Hueneme, California, together enjoy the advantage of having the only deep-water harbor between Los Angeles and San Francisco. The newspapers in Los Angeles and Oxnard emphasize this as a special influence which attracts manufacturing plants to locate near this facility. Manufacturing plants employ people, and people need homes to live in and stores to provide goods and services.

Due to the spillover of population from Los Angeles, and to this special influence, Oxnard is one of the fastest growing cities in California.

A small syndicate of which I am a member owns property in Oxnard, which was acquired because of the favorable growth factor as reported in the news media.

We have an office subscription to the local newspaper, and screen it carefully for news which might affect the property which is located there. Annexations to the city, rezoning, new construction, new manufacturing plants, all these are important influences, and information about them should be kept available.

Keep a scrapbook of favorable news items to assist in attracting investors to join in a real estate syndicate in the area.

KEEP PROSPECTS INFORMED

Prospective investors want to be continuously informed that a syndicator is working seriously to form a real estate syndicate when the right property is found. Tell them, from time to time, something of the type of properties which have already been listed.

I have found, when keeping contact with prospective investors, that they might be satisfied with a somewhat smaller return if a project could be activated sooner.

The prospective investors who are keen to join in a real estate syndicate will keep their money in liquid, short-term investments in order to be ready to put up their share of the capital when needed.

A syndicator should keep his prospective investors informed, and should form a syndicate as soon as possible to keep the prospects lined up and ready to join the venture.

DANGLE THE BAIT OF BIGGER PROFITS

Real estate syndication is rapidly moving into a position which, in the field of real estate, is similar to that of mutual funds with relation to the stock market. Respected observers report that they believe that the total investment by participants in real estate syndicates rivals or exceeds the total investment by the public in mutual fund companies.

The variety of mutual fund companies and their objectives, and the many different types of real estate syndicates with their diverse aims, make comparisons difficult, but there can be no doubt that the income from a real estate syndicate can be much greater, and the potential for capital gain of well selected real estate far outstrips all other forms of investment.

A return of 8 to 10 per cent on invested capital is not unusual from commercial property, even without a mortgage to provide "leverage." Point this feature out to prospective investors who may presently be getting only 3 per cent or so as a return on investment stocks. Investors like the high returns which can be had by joining a real estate syndicate. Emphasize the high income to attract new investors.

DANGLE THE BAIT OF CAPITAL GAIN

Capital gain, with a potential which can far outstrip the gain from stocks, can be expected by those who join a real estate syndicate which is handled by an expert syndicator. Prices of certain vacant land can be expected to double in five years or so, and increases in rents can quickly push up the value of income property. There are good chances for capital gain in all parts of the United States where development is taking place, and this feature should be used to attract investors to join a real estate syndicate.

"TAX SHELTER"—DANGLE THIS BAIT

"Tax shelter" is a unique advantage which is available to owners of real estate, and which can be made available to those who join a real estate syndicate. This attraction is alone sufficient to command the interest of people with money to invest, and who are in high earning brackets. "Tax shelter" allows the investor to receive distributions of cash from a real estate syndicate, and to pay income tax on only a part of it at the time it is received. Later, when syndicate real estate is sold, the favorable long term capital gains treatment applies to any profit made on the resale.

POINTS TO KEEP IN MIND

√ A Syndicator seeking to find and attract investors must "get the word out" among the most likely prospective investors that he plans to form a real estate syndicate.

√ He must contact prospective investors and educate them with factual material about real estate syndication, the high profits to be made and the tax advantages to be gained.

√ Prospective investors who are properly briefed on the unusual profits to be made and the tax advantages of group buying of real estate will sell themselves on investing in a real estate syndicate.

CHAPTER 8—

Convincing Investors to

Join a Syndicate

Convincing investors to join a syndicate is a selling job. Anyone who has made a study of successful selling knows that the salesman must *convince* the buyer to act. The salesman cannot force the buyer to act; the buyer acts on his own volition when he is convinced.

Salesmen usually use "props" or tools to convince a buyer to act, printed matter supporting the statements of the salesman, and other items to convince the buyer of the advantage of owning the product.

A syndicator's "props" include a prospectus, evidences that other real estate syndicates have been successful and profitable, and some means of getting a commitment from the prospective syndicate investor when he is convinced of the merit of the proposed real estate syndication.

The proper presentation of the workings of a real estate syndicate by the syndicator to a prospective investor, outlining the full details by means of a prospectus which shows how a sample deal would work out, constitutes the salesmanship which is expected to bring the prospect to the point where he will volunteer to join in the venture.

These are the syndicator's convincers:
- The Prospectus.
- The Letter of Intent.

THE PROSPECTUS

There are some syndicators who operate without supporting data of any kind, and many have been very successful, the lawyer syndicator mentioned in Chapter 7 being an example. The average syndicator, however, needs the support of factual material to enable him to give a prospective syndicate investor the incentive to join in a syndication.

I believe in setting out the full details of any financial transaction with which I am connected, using supporting data as a device to excite the interest of a prospective investor, and a well-worked-out presentation of the data to convince him to act, to join in the venture. Anyone who joins in with me gets full and complete details covering all facets of the proposal, so that he can make a fair judgment of its merits before investing his money or committing himself in any way.

Real estate syndication has been big business in a number of the Eastern states, and for this reason they have enacted legislation for the guidance and regulation of syndicators, and for the protection of investors. New York, New Jersey, Pennsylvania, Illinois and many other states have covered this field of investment, and have enacted clear-cut laws and regulations with regard to the "public" aspects of this business activity. Most other states have no specific laws concerning real estate syndication. They rely on the real estate brokerage laws, the security laws and acts, to handle the matter until the activity grows.

Any sincere syndicator would want to present all of the details of a contemplated "private" real estate syndicate, preferably in the form of a prospectus.

I would prepare a prospectus similar to the sample, Exhibit 8-1, when forming a "private" real estate syndicate. I would then seek competent legal and tax counsel and submit the proposed prospectus for review and advice. I would accept advice with reference to the local and federal laws, and consider advice with reference to matters which are a businessman's concern.

SAMPLE PROSPECTUS

2800 East Main Street Associates

A Limited Partnership, Formed for Group Acquisition of the Property Commonly Known as 2800-04 East Main Street and 2784-87 Thompson Boulevard, Ventura, California.

Participating Limited Partnership Interests will not be publicly offered.

EXHIBIT 8-1

58

CONTENTS OF PROSPECTUS

1. Synopsis of Transaction

    a. Name of partnership and purpose thereof

    b. The property

    c. Priority of distributions

    d. Tax status

    e. Management of property

    f. How title is to be held

    g. Information about general partners

    h. The contract to purchase the property

    i. The general partners, their fiduciary relationship, financial interest, fees, charges and profits in the management and promotion of the venture

    j. Funds contributed, handling and return if transaction not completed

    k. Financial reports and tax returns

    l. Amount of capital to be raised

    m. Amount of capital to be contributed for each unit of Limited Partnership Interest

2. Limited partnership agreement

3. Description of the property

4. Lease details

5. Distributions to partners

6. Tax status

7. Letter of intent

EXHIBIT 8-1 (CON'T)

1. SYNOPSIS OF TRANSACTION

a. *2800 EAST MAIN STREET ASSOCIATES*, a California Limited Partnership, hereinafter referred to as the Partnership, has been formed to acquire fee ownership of the land and building at 2800-04 East Main Street, and 2783-87 Thompson Boulevard, Ventura, California.

b. *The Property*, 2800-04 East Main Street and 2783-87 Thompson Boulevard is a one-story commercial building containing six individual stores, all leased, on a lot approximately 50′ × 112′, with automobile parking supplied by the Ventura Parking District No. 2. (For complete descriptive statement see "Description of Property" and "Lease Details.")

c. *Anticipated priority of distributions.* Subject to conditions hereinafter set forth, the Partnership intends to make monthly distributions to limited partners commencing 45 days after close of escrow, at which time title to the Property is to be conveyed to the Partnership. The General Partnership interests are subordinate as to distributions from income of the Property, and as to distributions in the event of sale of the Property during the term of this Partnership as explained in Limited Partnership Agreement.

d. *Tax status.* Based on the present Internal Revenue Code and Regulations, it is estimated that a part of the net income of the Property will not be subject to ordinary income tax, and this will affect the tax status of distributions as explained under "Tax Status."

e. *Management of Property.* The Property will be managed by John J. Jones Real Estate. John J. Jones is one of the General Partners in the Partnership. Mr. Jones will be paid a management fee equal to 5% of the gross rents collected, for his services as manager of the Property.

f. *How Title Is to Be Held.* Title to the Property is to be held by the Partnership in fee ownership.

g. *Information About General Partners.* John J. Jones and Samuel S. Smith are the two General Partners of 2800 East Main Street Associates, a Limited Partnership.

   John J. Jones is a real estate broker, licensed by the State of California. He is 41 years of age, married, has two children and lives with his family at 223 Westway Boulevard, Ventura, California. Mr. Jones has successfully operated a general real estate business at 22 "A" Street, Ventura, for the past ten years. His office presently manages a number of apartment and commercial properties in the city.

   Samuel S. Smith is a businessman, owner of Business Machines Co., handling sales of office machines, stationery and supplies, at 1200 Main Street, Ventura. He is 40 years old, married, has one child, lives with his family at 1200 Leucadia Drive, Ventura, California. Mr. Smith has been in his present business in Ventura for the past twenty years.

h. *The Contract to Purchase the Property.* Samuel S. Smith has entered into a contract to purchase, for himself or assignee, the property at 2800-04 East Main Street and 2783-87 Thompson Boulevard, Ventura, California, from William G. and Fanny M. Ames, at a price of $175,000. Mr. Smith is to take title to the property subject to a First Trust Deed in the amount of $100,000, with interest to be paid at the rate of $6\frac{1}{2}\%$ per annum, monthly installments of principal and interest to be $675 each month for 25 years. The loan will be made by Mortgage Corp., with Superior Insurance Co., holder of the present loan on the property, as the lender. The purchase contract is dated September 1, 1967, and provides for an escrow

EXHIBIT 8-1 (CON'T)

which is to close on or before January 2, 1968. Earnest money deposit made by Mr. Smith is in the amount of $5,000. Pro-rations of taxes and other usual items will be as of the closing date. Seller pays usual expenses of the sale, and buyer pays for one-half the escrow fee, recording and other minor items usually paid by a buyer.

The seller, Mr. and Mrs. William G. Ames, and his real estate broker, George K. Doe, have no connection whatsoever with the Partnership, and no relations with either of the General Partners. Mr. John J. Jones is the real estate broker of record for the buyer, Samuel S. Smith, and the seller will pay him a commission amounting to $4,375, equal to one-half of the 5% brokerage commission, when and if the transaction is consummated. The Purchase Contract recites that the buyer, Samuel S. Smith, is acting for a Limited Partnership to be formed, and that he will be a General Partner in said Partnership, together with John J. Jones.

The buyer is to pay cash for the equity, in the amount of $75,000 (more or less due to pro-rations), and in the event that the buyer is unable to close the escrow on or before January 2, 1968, then the Contract will be voided, the sum of $1,000 will be forfeited to the seller, and the balance of the earnest money will be returned to the buyer.

i. *The General Partners—Relations With Partnership.* The fiduciary relationship of the General Partners to the Partnership is fully set forth in the sample Partnership Agreement which is a part of this Prospectus.

Samuel S. Smith and John J. Jones will each make a capital contribution of $100 in cash to the Partnership, Samuel S. Smith will assign his Contract to Purchase the Property to the Partnership and John J. Jones will contract to manage the property. They will each get a General Partnership Interest in the Partnership for their contributions. The General Partner's share of the profits from operation of the Property, the proceeds of sale or refinancing of the Property, will be as set forth in the Partnership Agreement, but will be subordinated to distributions to the Limited Partners as agreed.

Samuel S. Smith will make a capital contribution of $5,000 in cash to the Partnership for a Limited Partnership therein.

John J. Jones will make a capital contribution of $5,000 in cash to the Partnership for a Limited Partnership therein.

The General Partners are to be reimbursed for the actual out-of-pocket costs of organizing the Partnership, including attorney's fees, advertising, filing fees, setup of records by accountant, assignment of Contract to Purchase, and all other organizational expenses to set up the Partnership. This cost is estimated to be approximately $3,000.

Fees for any refinancing to be done, and commissions which the Partnership may be expected to pay for the resale of the Property, as outlined in the Agreement, will be charged in accordance with local custom. John J. Jones, one of the General Partners, will act as the exclusive agent for the Partnership, with the agreement to share commissions with cooperating brokers.

j. *Funds Contributed—Handling and Return If Transaction Is Not Completed.* All funds contributed by Limited Partners, and all funds contributed by General Partners, shall be held as trust funds in a special bank account to be applied toward the consummation of the contemplated transaction.

In the event that the total amount to be raised, namely $80,200.00, is not available

EXHIBIT 8-1 (CON'T)

to consummate the transaction on or before January 2, 1968, then all funds which have been deposited shall be refunded in full to the parties who made the contributions, without deduction, but without payment of any interest thereon.

k. *Financial Reports and Tax Returns.* A copy of the real estate manager's monthly rent statement showing rent income of the Property, and operating expenses paid out of said rents, together with a statement showing cash on hand at the end of each month, shall be forwarded to each Limited Partner within 15 days after the end of each calendar month. An annual report, prepared by a public accountant, together with "Information on State and Federal Partnership" income tax returns covering operations of the Partnership, and a computation showing the portion of the cash distribution which would be subject to individual income tax by the Limited Partners, will be forwarded to them within 10 days after the end of each calendar year. Accounting costs are estimated at $300 per annum. Costs of monthly reports will be nominal.

l. *Amount of Capital to be Raised.* The amount of capital to be raised by cash contributions from Limited Partners will be $80,000.00. The amount of capital to be raised by cash contributions from the General Partners will be $200.00. Total cash capital to be raised, $80,200.00.

m. *Use of Proceeds.* The cash proceeds, consisting of the contributions to capital by the Limited and General Partners, in the total amount of $80,200.00, will be applied toward the consummation of the transaction as follows : $5,000.00 to reimburse Samuel S. Smith for the deposit advanced by him on account of the Purchase Contract ; $70,000, for payment of the balance of the purchase price, (more or less due to pro-rations of taxes, etc.); approximately $3,000.00 as reimbursement to Samuel S. Smith for the actual out-of-pocket expenses of forming the Partnership and organization thereof; the balance of approximately $2,000.00 to be deposited in a separate Partnership bank account as working surplus.

n. *Amount of Capital to Be Contributed for Each Uuit of Limited Partnership Interest.* A unit of Limited Partnership can be acquired by making a cash contribution of capital in the amount of $5,000.00 to the Partnership.

The General Partners may, at their sole discretion, provide that units of Limited Partnership interest be issued with contributions of capital to be made to the Partnership of multiples of $5,000, or for amounts less than $5,000.

EXHIBIT 8-1 (CON'T)

2. LIMITED PARTNERSHIP AGREEMENT

<u>2800 EAST MAIN STREET ASSOCIATES</u>
(Partnership Name)

<u> </u>
(Effective Date of Agreement)

AGREEMENT OF LIMITED PARTNERSHIP FOR GROUP ACQUISITION OF THE PROPERTY COMMONLY KNOWN AS <u>2800-04 EAST MAIN STREET and 2784-87 THOMPSON BOULEVARD, VENTURA, CALIFORNIA.</u>

I

NAME AND DATE   The name and effective date of this limited partnership shall be as set forth in the caption above.

II

PURPOSE   The purpose of this limited partnership is to acquire for investment the real property described above.

III

PRINCIPAL OFFICE   The principal office of this limited partnership shall be at the business office of the first general partner undersigned.

IV

TERM   The term of this limited partnership shall begin as of its effective date and shall end twenty-one (21) years thereafter, or sooner, as provided below.

V

CAPITAL   Each limited partner shall contribute as capital the sum set opposite his name. All sums deposited shall be returned to each limited partner on or before one hundred twenty (120) days after the effective date of this agreement if the total of all limited partners' capital contributions do not equal the sum of $80,000.00 by said date.

VI

PROFITS   80% of partnership profits and losses shall be credited to limited partners on December 31 of each year in the same ratio of their capital balances. The balance of partnership profits or losses shall be credited to the general partners. Depreciation shall be allocated in the same ratio as partners' share of profits and losses.

EXHIBIT 8-1 (CON'T)

VII

PRIORITY Notwithstanding the division of profits set forth in paragraph VI, all partnership profits up to 9% per annum of each limited partner's original capital account, as reduced by proceeds of any refinancing of partnership property, shall be credited to each limited partner's capital account if greater than the amount provided for in paragraph VI. This provision shall not be cumulative from year to year. The term "profits" as used in this agreement shall be the amount reported by the partnership for federal income tax purposes exclusive of depreciation. Cash distributions shall be made at least annually in the same ratio as partners share profits and losses as set forth in paragraph VI.

VIII

SALE The net proceeds from any sale of partnership property shall be distributed in the following order :

(a) To each limited partner up to the balance of his capital account, exclusive of depreciation ;

(b) To each general partner up to the balance of his capital account, exclusive of accumulated depreciation ;

(c) To the general partners up to the sum of $20,000.00 ;

(d) To the limited partners and to the general partners in the same ratio as they share profits as set forth in paragraph VI.

IX

LOSSES Limited partners shall not be responsible for losses in excess of their capital balances.

X

MANAGEMENT The general partners shall be responsible to manage the partnership property. Five (5%) per cent of the gross income received shall be paid to the general partners for management services.

XI

PROPERTY ACQUISITION General partners shall sell all their title and interest in the above-described property to the partnership at the time that all partnership funds have been received according to the terms of the deposit receipt attached.

XII

LIMITED PARTNERS Limited partners shall not participate in the management of partnership affairs, shall not receive property other than cash in return for capital contributions, and shall not have priority over other limited partners with respect to distributions of capital or profits. No additional limited partners may be admitted to the partnership.

EXHIBIT 8-1 (CON'T)

XIII

REFINANCING AND SALES The general partners may refinance and/or obtain additional loans secured by partnership property. Net proceeds from any refinancing of partnership property shall be distributed among the partners in the same ratio as the partners share profits and losses as set forth in paragraph VI. The general partners may sell partnership property on behalf of the partnership for such terms and conditions as they determine in their discretion, provided that the net cash proceeds from any sale is sufficient to return to each limited partner in cash the balance of his capital account. The general partners shall be entitled to receive customary commissions for any refinancing or sale of partnership property.

XIV

SIGNATURES Any deed, deed of trust, lease, contract of sale, bill of sale, or other similar document shall be executed by each general partner; no other signatures shall be required.

XV

BOOKS Partnership books shall be kept at its principal office and shall be open for inspection by all partners. The partnership books shall be closed at the end of each calendar year; the federal and state income tax returns required shall be prepared by a public accountant employed by the partnership.

XVI

ASSIGNMENT OF INTEREST A limited partner shall not substitute a new limited partner or assign his interest in the partnership without first obtaining the written consent of all the general partners.

XVII

DEATH OF LIMITED PARTNER The interest of a deceased limited partner shall pass to his estate. The death of a limited partner shall not dissolve or terminate the partnership business.

XVIII

DISSOLUTION The partnership shall dissolve prior to the end of its term on the sale of the entire partnership property, or in the event of the death, bankruptcy or incompetency of a general partner. Upon the dissolution of the partnership, the surviving general partners shall have the right, without the obligation, to form a new limited partnership to engage in the same business as this partnership, and to employ the assets and the name of this partnership. Each limited partner by execution of this agreement appoints the general partners and each of them as his attorney-in-fact to record a new certificate of limited partnership following the dissolution and termination of this partnership. The surviving general partners shall record a new certificate of limited partnership as attorney-in-fact for each of the limited partners in the event of dissolution and termination, and in such event the assets and liabilities of this partnership shall be assigned to and be assumed by such new limited partnership. The general partners shall record a new certificate of limited partnership containing provisions substantially the same as those appearing in the certificate

EXHIBIT 8-1 (CON'T)

of limited partnership recorded for this partnership, except that the term of the new partnership shall expire on the date which is not beyond the date that this partnership would expire by a lapse of time. The general partners shall give written notice whether or not a new limited partnership shall be formed to each limited partner at their respective addresses appearing in the partnership records within three (3) months after the event causing the dissolution of the partnership.

XIX

INDEMNITY   The partnership shall indemnify any general partner for personal loss or damage for reason of any act performed on behalf of the partnership and in the furtherance of its interest.

XX

BINDING   This agreement shall inure to and bind all of the parties, their estates, heirs, personal representatives and assigns.

XXI

COUNTER-PARTS   This agreement may be executed in counterparts, all of which taken together shall be deemed one original agreement.

XXII

CAPTIONS   Paragraph titles or captions in no way define, limit, extend, or describe the scope of this agreement nor the intent of any provision thereof.

GENERAL PARTNERS:

Name	Business Office	Contribution
_____	_____	$_____
_____	_____	_____

LIMITED PARTNERS:

Name	Business Office	Contribution
_____	_____	$_____
_____	_____	_____

EXHIBIT 8-1 (CON'T)

3. DESCRIPTION OF PROPERTY

<u>2800-02-04 EAST MAIN STREET</u> and

<u>2783-85-87 THOMPSON BOULEVARD</u>

VENTURA, CALIFORNIA

EXCELLENT STRATEGICALLY LOCATED BUSINESS PROPERTY * * * * *

LOCATION: In the very active Buena Center Shopping District of East Ventura, where most of the building activity in and around Ventura has taken place and will continue to take place. This property is located in the same block and on the same side of the street as the Sears Roebuck Store, which store, we understand is to be enlarged in the near future. It also adjoins a large Rasco 10¢ to $1.00 store.

LAND &
  BUILDING: There is a frontage on both East Main Street and Thompson Boulevard of about 50' and a depth between the two streets of 112'. Zone CI-A.

Improvements consist of a very fine one-story concrete block, stud and stucco building covering the entire lot and containing five units, two of which face on East Main Street and three on Thompson Boulevard. The building is of steel beam and laminated wood beam construction, with interior walls of lath and plaster. Exterior walls are of cement stucco. Ceilings are finished with acoustical plaster. Each unit is equipped with American Standard plumbing, time clocks for window and outside light control, and there are six Lennox 3 H.P. heat pumps for air-conditioning and heating. Fronts are of plate glass, Alumalited aluminum, and imported Venetian tile. Aluminum entrance doors have plate glass panels and floor door checks. Fine fluorescent light fixtures provide 30 Lumens at desk height, and there is vinyl-asbestos tile floor covering.

INCOME: GROSS ANNUAL RENTAL (Average)............................$21,600.00

EXPENSES:

(*Estimated*)		
General Taxes	$1,384.68	
Insurance	334.63	
Water	70.00	
Janitor Service—Metro Life	840.00	
Electricity—Metro Life	851.02	
Management—5% × $21,600	1,080.00	4,560.33

APPROX. NET INCOME (Based on clear bldg.)		$17,039.67
LOAN: $100,000—6½%—25 years.—$675 Mo.—Interest Only		6,500.00
ANNUAL NET INCOME		$10,539.67
Equity Buildup (Principal Payment) 1st year		1,600.00
"Cash Flow" on $75,000 equity = 11.9%.....................		$ 8,939.67

EXHIBIT 8-1 (CON'T)

4. LEASE DETAILS

ITEMIZED RENTS AND LEASE MATURITIES
2800–02–04 EAST MAIN STREET AND
2783–85–87 THOMPSON BOULEVARD, VENTURA.

EAST MAIN STREET

2800–02	Metropolitan Life Insurance Company, (2 stores re-modeled into offices.) Rental $650 per month	$ 650.00
2804	Mercantile Acceptance Company of San Francisco, D/B/A Laurentide Finance Co. This is a loan concern dealing in auto and small personal loans. They have some 250 offices in United States and Canada. Rental $300 per month	300.00

THOMPSON BOULEVARD

2783	Gude's Junior Bootery. Rental 6% of sales with minimum guaranteed rental of $275 per month	275.00
2785	Norman P. Cowan. Barber supplies and cosmetics. Graduated rental–Average rental during 5 year period	300.00
2787	Odell's Children's Wear. Rental 5% of gross annual sales. Minimum guaranteed rental $275 per month	275.00
	Total Average Monthly Rental..................	$ 1,800.00
	TOTAL AVERAGE YEARLY RENTAL..............	$21,600.00

EXHIBIT 8-1 (CON'T)

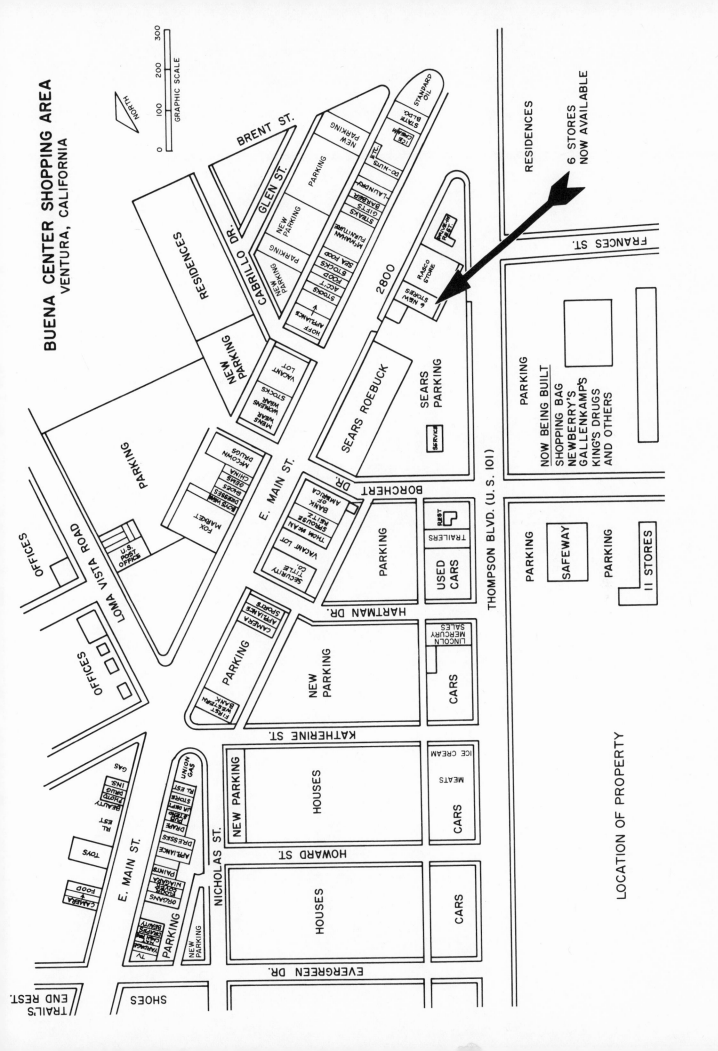

BUENA CENTER SHOPPING AREA
VENTURA, CALIFORNIA

NORTH

GRAPHIC SCALE
0 100 200 300

LOCATION OF PROPERTY

6 STORES NOW AVAILABLE

RESIDENCES

FRANCES ST.

NOW BEING BUILT
SHOPPING BAG
NEWBERRY'S
GALLENKAMP'S
KING'S DRUGS
AND OTHERS

PARKING

PARKING

SAFEWAY

PARKING

11 STORES

THOMPSON BLVD. (U.S. 101)

RASCO STORE

6 NEW STORES

2800

WESTERN REST.

STATE BLDG.

STANDARD OIL

ICE CREAM

DO-NUTS

LAUNDRY

BARBER

GIFTS

STEAKS

McMAHAN FURNITURE

SEA FOOD

FOOD

ACC'T

STOCKS

HOPF APPLIANCE

NEW PARKING

PARKING

NEW PARKING

GLEN ST.

BRENT ST.

CABRILLO DR.

RESIDENCES

NEW PARKING

VACANT LOT

STOCKS

WOMENS WEAR

MENS WEAR

SEARS ROEBUCK

SEARS PARKING

SERVICE

BORCHERT DR.

MCCOWN DRUGS

CHINA

GEMS

SHOES

DRESSES

BOYS WEAR

FOX MARKET

E. MAIN ST.

SECURITY TITLE CO.

VACANT LOT

THOM McAN

SPROUSE REITZ

BANK OF AMERICA

REST.

TRAILERS

PARKING

USED CARS

LINCOLN MERCURY SALES

CARS

HARTMAN DR.

CAMERA

APPLIANCE

SPORTS

FIRST WESTERN BANK

PARKING

NEW PARKING

KATHERINE ST.

HOUSES

NEW PARKING

MEATS

ICE CREAM

CARS

OFFICES

PARKING

LOMA VISTA ROAD

U.S. POST OFFICE

OFFICES

BEAUTY

R.E. EST

PHOTO DRUG INS.

GAS

TOYS

R.E. EST

UNION GAS

RL. EST.

LN DEPT. STORE

PHOTO

DRAPE

DRESSES

APPLIANCE

ORGANS

BOOKS

PAINTS

DOVER

NIAGARA

CAMERA

FOOD

BEAUTY

DRESS

CAFE

DRAPES

CLOTHIER

TV

E. MAIN ST.

PARKING

NEW PARKING

NICHOLAS ST.

HOUSES

HOWARD ST.

CARS

EVERGREEN DR.

TRAIL'S END REST.

SHOES

5. NET INCOME CREDITED TO PARTNERS' ACCOUNTS   6. TAX STATUS

	Total	80% to Limited Partners' Accounts	20% to General Partners' Accounts
Net Income	$10,539.67	$8,431.74	$2,107.93
Depreciation	4,000.00	3,200.00	800.00
Taxable	$ 6,539.67	$5,231.74	$1,307.93

Distributable "Cash Flow"

	Total	80%	20%
Net Income	$10,539.67	$8,431.74	$2,107.93
Mortgage Payoff	1,600.00	1,280.00	320.00
"Cash Flow"	$ 8,939.67	$7,151.74	$1,787.93

*Net Income on $5,000 Limited Partnership Interest

Net Income on $5,000 share

   5% × $10,539.67 $ 530.00 = 10.5% earned.

Depreciation = 5% × $4,000.00   200.00

Taxable $ 330.00

Cash Distribution on $5,000 Limited Partnership Interest

Cash Distribution on $5,000

   share—1/16th × $7,151.74 $ 447.00 = 8.94%

Taxable   330.00

"Tax Shelter" $ 117.00

*Rounded to even dollars.

EXHIBIT 8-1 (CON'T)

LETTER OF INTENT

To Mr. John J. Jones and
Mr. Samuel S. Smith,
c/o John J. Jones, Real Estate,
22 " A " Street,
Ventura, California.

Gentlemen:

With this letter I declare my intention to join in a real estate syndicate for the purchase of income real estate in or near the City of Ventura.

I understand that the property to be purchased will be owned by a Limited Partnership, that you will be the General Partners, further that the partnership Agreement and details of the transaction will be approximately as set forth in a sample prospectus which was exhibited to me for my inspection.

Provided that the property to be acquired is to my satisfaction, and that other details of the transaction are as represented, I would be interested in acquiring a Limited Partnership Interest, for a cash contribution to the partnership of the sum of $5,000.00.

This expression of intent, subject to my approval of the contemplated transaction, is for the purpose of enabling you to work out the details of said real estate syndicate, and will become null and void and of no effect Ninety (90) Days after date of this letter.

Dated at _____, _____ 19 _____

_____
Signature

_____
Address

_____
City & State

EXHIBIT 8-1 (CON'T)

POINTS TO KEEP IN MIND

√ The prospectus, a sample of which is shown as Figure 8-1, is the best tool which a syndicator can use to convince investors to join a real estate syndicate.

√ The prospectus should contain factual information which emphasizes the profit potential for the participating investors.

√ The prospectus must completely detail the position of the syndicator, and give every detail of the compensation which is to accrue to the syndicator, directly or indirectly by reason of his connection with, organization, and operation of a real estate syndicate which might be formed at a later date.

√ A prospective participating investor would want to know that the factual material describing the property, which is the basic example for the sample prospectus, concerns a real property similar to that which might later be syndicated.

√ Some syndicators use a "Letter of Intent" to commit prospective investors to some degree, but usually only on advice of legal counsel.

CHAPTER 9—

Types of Organization

There are a number of different types of organizations which have been used as the business vehicle for real estate syndication. Real estate syndicates have also been successfully operated with no business organization of any kind, the real estate being owned by the members of the syndicate as tenants in common, holding title to undivided fractional interests.

The syndicator, as a businessman, must evaluate the various forms of organization and methods of handling the business of a real estate syndicate to determine which type is most adaptable to the situation, and to his objectives.

The manner in which a syndicate is to be organized depends on a number of factors, the main ones being the relationship of the members of the syndicate to each other, the effect of income taxes on the profits, and the capability of making the best use of "tax-shelter" for the benefit of the members of the real estate syndicate.

I give you two principal methods of handling the business of a real estate syndicate, a list of the various types of organization which may be used with each method, and my comments about each.

- *Holding title to the real estate* in such a way that division of profits or losses is dependent on evidences of fractional ownership of the property.
- Use of a recognized business organization, formed in accordance with the business activity laws of the federal government and the state in which the business is to be conducted. The type of business selected is to be the one which is the business vehicle for the real estate syndicate.

The most commonly used variations of each method are enumerated and described, with comments.

THE TITLE HOLDING METHOD TYPES

1. Holding title to real estate with the members of the real estate syndicate as tenants in common, each holding title to an undivided fractional interest in the property.
2. Tenancy in common (same as No. 1), with the addition of a simple agreement among the title holders as syndicate members. (See Exhibit 9-1, Agreement Between Tenants in Common.)
3. Use of a "dummy" as title holder of the property. The "dummy" owner gives the other members of the syndicate group a letter, an agreement, or a partial deed to show their interest in the property. The deed is not to be recorded.
4. Use of a "title holding trust." With this arrangement a "trustee" takes title to the real estate of a syndicate group, governed by a simple "trust agreement." Evidence of fractional ownership of the real estate is set forth by naming the individuals as beneficiaries of the "trust". The "trustee" has very limited powers, usually only to hold title, execute documents such as leases or mortgages, and to deal with the title as directed by the beneficiaries.

Operation of the real estate is by one or more of the beneficiaries, or by a delegated managing agent. Beneficiaries can transfer all or part of their beneficial interests in the trust by giving directions to the trustee. The trustee can be an individual, or a trust company. The usual trust agreement cannot cover all of the detailed business arrangements of a real estate syndicate without assuming the risk of being classified as a corporation for income tax purposes. A limited partnership might use a trustee to hold title. A trust company holding title to syndicated real estate instills confidence in investors.

EXHIBIT 9-1

MEMORANDUM OF AGREEMENT BETWEEN TENANTS IN COMMON

This shall serve as a memorandum of an agreement between

_____ , _____

_____ and _____ .

I

Purpose

The parties agree to purchase as co-owners and as tenants in common certain improved property commonly known as _____ Street, in the City of _____ County of _____ and State of _____ , described in the exhibit attached, hereafter called the "Property," to hold the same for investment purposes.

II

Participation

Profits and losses, contributions, and distributions with respect to the Property are to be shared equally by all of the parties.

III

Failure to Contribute

In the event that one or more parties shall fail to make their proportionate share of required contributions for the initial down payment, the periodic payments of principal or interest, taxes or other expenses as required, then the other parties shall have an equal right and option to make up such sums in default, and in the event that the party in default fails to cure such default, within thirty (30) days after such payment in default was due, then the other parties having cured the default shall have the option to purchase the interest in the Property of the party in default using the same procedures to determine the price and terms as set froth in Sec IV, hereof.

IV

Death of a Party

In the event that a party dies while all or any portion of the Property remains unsold, the surviving parties shall have an equal and exclusive option for a period of sixty (60) days after the death of such party to purchase from his estate all of his title and interest in the Property by giving a written notice of election to the personal representative of the estate of such deceased party, or to a known heir of such deceased party if no personal representative be appointed. The option price shall be the total disbursements made by the deceased party prior to his death with respect to the Property, including the down payment, principal and interest payments, and taxes, provided, that from time to time the parties may by a mutual agreement stipulate to a fair market value for the Property, and such stipulation shall be made in all events following any sale of any portion of the Property, and thereupon for purposes of this paragraph the option price shall be the decedent's share of the fair market value of the Property determined by subtracting all encumbrances and liabilities against the Property from such stipulated fair market value. The purchase price shall be paid in cash at the time the option is exercised.

V

First Refusal

A party desiring to sell all or any part of his undivided interest in the Property shall first present to the other parties the proposed offer or agreement of sale, and for ten (10) days thereafter the other parties shall have equal and exclusive option to purchase such interest upon the same terms and conditions as set forth in said offer or agreement of sale, such option to be exercised by delivering to the party desiring to sell a notice in writing of such election, and if such option is not exercised within the time allowed, the party desiring to sell shall obtain in writing an acknowledgement from the other parties that such offer or agreement of sale had been presented to them and had been declined.

VI

Management

Unanimous agreement of the parties shall be required for the improvement, development or sale of the Property.

VII

Title

Title shall be held as tenants in common.

Modifications

All modifications of this agreement shall become effective only when reduced to writing and signed by the parties.

Dated : _____

                             _____

                             _____

                             _____

                             _____

Exhibit 9-1 (Continued)

Advantages of title holding methods

Holding title as tenants in common is simple, and easily understood by those who join a group to syndicate real estate. They get a deed, which is recorded, showing their fractional interest in the property. An extra agreement can be drawn to cover division of profits and losses and other details of the deal. (See Exhibit 9-1.)

Use of a "dummy" to hold title has the advantage that the "dummy" appears as the owner of record. Dealing with the property is simplified. The interests of others as owners of fractional interests are not disclosed.

Use of a title holding trust provides the same advantages as the use of a "dummy" title holder. In addition, if the trustee is a bank or title company, investors are inclined to believe that they have a greater security of their capital investment, since the trustee deals with refinancing of the real estate, and with the title, at the direction of the beneficiaries. Beneficial interests can be transferred by direction of the beneficiary involved. The beneficiaries get a copy of the trust agreement showing their fractional interest in the trust which owns the real estate. The names of the beneficiaries may not be disclosed.

Disadvantages of title holding methods

Holding title as tenants in common, the death of any co-owner, divorce proceedings or other litigation against any one of them, or a disagreement among them could cause delays in dealing with the property, possibly interfere with the management of the real estate and the disposition of the income, or cause a forced sale of the holding.

Use of a "dummy" as title holder for a syndicate group entails obvious risks. The "dummy" is the owner of record, and could deal with the property without the consent of the other members of the owning group. He could rent or sell the property, mortgage it, or divert the income. The other members of the group would have to sue him to enforce any agreement made with him. The co-owners would probably have no recourse against third parties with whom the "dummy" owner dealt with regard to the co-owned property, unless a fraud or conspiracy could be proved. The death or divorce of the "dummy" title holder or litigation against him could cause serious difficulties for the syndicate group.

Use of a title holding trust usually requires that a supplementary agreement be drawn to outline the arrangements made for co-ownership of the property. This agreement must be carefully considered, and so drawn that the trust agreement and the operating agreement do not together encompass all of the characteristics of a corporation, with resultant high income tax liabilities.

The best choice for a trustee is a trust company which is also a bank or title company. An individual as trustee can cause problems similar to those encountered with a "dummy" title holder.

THE RECOGNIZED BUSINESS ORGANIZATION TYPES

The five types of recognized business organization which are most commonly used as the business framework for a real estate syndicate are as follows, with my comments about each.

- The Partnership
- The Limited Partnership
- The Joint Venture
- The Real Estate Investment Trust
- The Corporation

Each of these types of business organization is subject to the business activity laws and regulations of the state in which it operates, and to some extent to regulation by the federal government.

THE PARTNERSHIP

Usually described as the general partnership, it is probably the best known form of business structure. Simply stated, a general partnership consists of two or more persons who agree to pool capital and talents to conduct a business activity, and to divide profits and losses on an agreed basis. The partners each have rights to commit the partnership to certain obligations, unless these rights are restricted by the agreement. All partners are liable for the obligations of the partnership.

A general partnership, with the agreement properly drawn, can work out as the business vehicle for a real estate syndicate.

There are income tax advantages which can accrue to the members of a real estate syndicate when a partnership is used as the business vehicle. The advantages are that the partnership pays no income taxes, and it can pass along to the partners the profits, losses, depreciation, capital gain and losses, for use in the individual partner's income tax return.

To be classed as a partnership for income tax purposes, the partnership agreement must be drawn to avoid including all of the characteristics of a corporation. The four attributes which are the test of a corporation are lack of personal liability, continuity, centralized management and transferability of certificates of interest.

There are a number of ways in which most of the qualities of a corporation can be had without sacrificing the benefits of a partnership. This is usually achieved through restrictions, which permit the partners to have and exercise the desirable rights and exemptions which they would have with a corporation, but stipulate that some of the attributes can only be enjoyed by permission of the other partners, or, preferably, by delegating some of the privileges to others.

For instance, a general partnership can own real estate and lease it to the syndicator. Then the partnership has no centralized management. Distribution of rent paid to the partnership by the syndicator is not considered to be management. Certain vital decisions can still be left to the partnership, such as refinancing or sale of the property.

The partners can still have personal liability, but the hazards can be fully insured, and with the syndicator operating the real estate, and also carrying insurance, the liabilities are minimized.

The partnership agreement could now provide for continuity of the partnership, and transferability of the interests, because these two similarities to a corporation would be the only ones included.

Advantages of a general partnership

The legal background of the general partnership as a type of business organization is well established. The use of general partnerships has been so common that practically all legal problems which arise have been resolved, and attorneys can recommend this type of organization because of this.

Most people know something about partnerships, and they are attracted by the fact that they would have a voice in the management of the organization if they invest money in it.

There are income tax advantages where a general partnership is used as a vehicle for a real estate syndicate. The depreciation on improvements on real estate can be passed on to the partners to apply against their personal income taxes. Losses or carrying charges on the real estate can also be passed on to reduce the tax of the individual partner.

Disadvantages of a general partnership

There is no centralized management. Any partner can commit the partnership to obligate all of the partners. An agreement must be reached among the partners to divide up the work to be done by the partners.

There is no continuity of the organization. The death of any partner can cause the partnership to be dissolved.

There is no right to transfer individual partnership interests.

All partners have full personal liability for obligations of the partnership.

THE LIMITED PARTNERSHIP

This form of partnership has two classes of partners, the general partners, who manage the affairs of the partnership, and the limited partners, who invest money as silent partners, with no real voice in the management, and no personal liability beyond their investment.

A limited partnership, therefore, furnishes centralized management, which is a function of the general partners, and limited liability for the limited partners.

Transferability of limited partnership interests can be provided for, subject to consent of the general partners. A provision for continuing the partnership can be arranged.

The limited partnership thus appears reasonably to provide all four of the features which would make a corporation desirable, with certain tolerable modifications. The sample Limited Partnership Agreement (see Chapter 8) shows one way to draw such a document to get the most out of a real estate syndication.

Advantages

A carefully drawn limited partnership agreement can be simple, and still include most of the advantages of a corporation. The partnership pays no income taxes, but funnels to the partners the profits, depreciation and other items such as the expense of carrying vacant land, just as if they each owned a small parcel of real estate instead of their partnership interests.

In my opinion, the limited partnership, with a properly drawn agreement, can be the best vehicle for a real estate syndication.

Disadvantages

Care must be used in drafting the limited partnership agreement to avoid being classified as a corporation for income tax purposes. The general partners have liability for the obligations of the partnership. The other disadvantages are mostly in the minds of the participants, since sophisticated investors generally have a greater amount of confidence in a corporation.

THE JOINT VENTURE

The true joint venture has some of the characteristics of a partnership, but it is usually organized to be used for one deal only. Attorneys seem to think that the general and limited partnerships are more satisfactory for use because the many court decisions regarding the commonly used partnership organizations have made this form legally predictable.

The newspapers carry publications of Certificates of Joint Ventures, with real estate as the purpose, so that there must be situations where its use is desirable. A syndicator might consider using the joint venture as a vehicle for a real estate syndication if it appears to offer advantages over one of the partnership types.

THE REAL ESTATE INVESTMENT TRUST

This type of organization, permitted under federal law, is meant primarily for very large investments in real estate and has some advantages when used as the vehicle for a big deal.

The law requires that there be at least 100 investors. The formation of a real estate investment trust is complicated and takes some time.

This type of organization appears to be unsuitable for any but a very large operation.

THE CORPORATION

Whenever a group of people contemplate a business venture they think first of the corporation as the ideal organization for it.

The organizers of the business like the corporation because it provides limited liability for the whole group, centralized management, continuity, and transferability of certificates of interest. There is also glamour in the titles given to officers and directors. The corporation is easier to sell to investors because they have more confidence in such an organization than in less sophisticated types.

Other advantages are that investors like the corporation as the framework of a business venture because it provides them with limited liability and there is pride of possession of stock ownership. They also feel secure because the corporation is subject to regulatory laws, and some governmental supervision of its formation and operations.

Disadvantages of the corporation

Income taxes on the earnings of real estate which the corporation owns are high. The stockholders pay income taxes again on any dividends paid by the corporation to them. Depreciation, costs of carrying vacant land and operational losses are locked into the corporation and cannot be passed along to investors to reduce their taxable personal incomes. Capital gains would be taxed in the corporation and again when the investors divide the profit. The operation of a corporation requires that time-consuming records be kept, and complicated tax returns be made. The organization of a corporation is expensive, and dissolution is just as costly. Lenders want personal guarantees from the principals of small corporations. The waiver of such guarantees is negotiable, but could as easily be obtained for a partnership.

The thin corporation

This variation consists of a minimum of capital stock investment and a maximum of loans to the corporation by stockholders to supply cash needed to operate.

The problem with the thin corporation is that there is no positive way to determine the ratio of capital stock to loans which will be acceptable to the Internal Revenue Service. Its agents often claim that the loans are really capital investment and cash paid to the lenders as interest should be classed as dividends.

The thin corporation might be the one to use, but the risk is there. I prefer other organizational types.

The tax-sheltered corporation

The ideal tax-sheltered corporation would own real estate which has sufficient depreciation on improvements to offset its taxable income. Such a corporation could avoid income tax as long as the money paid out to investors could not be classed as "essentially equivalent" to a dividend. A corporation, under present tax laws, must have "earnings or profits" to pay a dividend.

It is my opinion that a syndicator should cautiously consider all of the merits and demerits of the corporate type of organization before deciding to use it as the vehicle for a real estate syndication.

POINTS TO KEEP IN MIND

√ A syndicator should give careful consideration to the type of property ownership or business organization which is to be the vehicle for a real estate syndication.

√ The ownership of real estate by title holding methods entails risks, and the lack of centralized control tends to make this type of ownership unsatisfactory for the purpose, except in unusual cases.

√ The corporation, a business organization which has much appeal for investors generally, is burdened with heavy taxes and other disadvantages which makes its use impractical as a vehicle for real estate syndication.

√ The limited partnership, making use of a carefully drawn agreement, appears to offer the most advantages to a syndicator who wants to get the most out of a real estate syndication for all participants.

CHAPTER 10—

How to Find the Investment

Assume that you have decided on the type, size and general locale of property which might be suitable for your syndicate. Also assume that you have determined the objectives of your syndication, which could be income, capital gain, prepaid interest, or a combination of these.

The problem of how to find the investment can now be solved by following the procedures which have proved successful over long years of my experience, a method which is used by most experienced real estate investors.

There are five basic steps to this method of hunting for, analyzing and choosing a property suitable for your syndicate. Follow these five steps and you will discover those properties which stand out and command your attention. From these few, you can easily select the one property which offers the best profit opportunities. The five key steps are:

- Get all obtainable listings of suitable properties in your area.
- Accumulate complete data on offerings of merit.
- Thoroughly analyze the data.
- Select the two best listings by process of elimination.
- Choose the one property which offers the greatest profit potential for your syndicate.

HOW TO GET ALL OBTAINABLE LISTINGS

Get zoning information and maps, a copy of the building code, and general or master planning material for your area of interest. These are inexpensive and invaluable tools which pinpoint the areas which are zoned for properties which might interest you. They give complete information with which to check the conformity of the property offered, and also give full information about permitted uses for that type of property. The master plan shows the proposed location of new highways, forecasts increases in population, business and industry trends and contains a wealth of other invaluable material. The federal government encourages local governments to make general or master plans, and, in fact, they are almost compelled to have such planning to get federal aid.

Study the maps and data to familiarize yourself with the areas which would be zoned for the property of interest to you, and to get a picture of the proposed public improvements which will accommodate the increased population and industry in a growth area.

Use the properties which you already know something about, the ones which probably attracted you to syndication, as a nucleus of listings. Get preliminary information about these properties as set forth in Exhibit 10-2, preliminary listing form. Make a personal inspection of the properties to supplement factual information with a visual impression.

Inspect the area surrounding these properties, and circle out far enough in all directions to get the feel of the neighborhood which supports the subject property. Be alert for influences which could be helpful, or detrimental to the property of interest.

Tour the other areas which are zoned for the purpose which you are interested in, and look for "For Sale" and "For Rent" signs, making note of those which might be of interest, either as prospective properties to buy, or as a comparison of rents being paid.

Your inspection tours will undoubtedly bring to your attention other properties which appear to fit the requirements of your syndicate. Make note of the addresses, and a sketchy description of the property, with your impressions of it. Consider all properties which could possibly be handled with the equity money which you expect to raise by syndication.

When you see a building or other property which interests you, find the owner's name and address. The most direct way to accomplish this is to ask the tenants or neighbors for the information, if there is no sign on the property giving the owner's name. Failing this, you can look up ownerships on the county records, or get them from a title company.

Contact these owners, ask if the property is for sale, and, if so, make a personal call to get information about it. In the event that the property is not for sale, ask if the owner knows of other similar property which might be in the market. This owner might have recently acquired the property after searching over the same area which you are working on.

Classified advertising sections of newspapers and real estate and building periodicals carry "Wanted to Buy" columns, and a small item inserted in one of these columns, listing your requirements, can produce surprising results.

Lending institutions, such as banks, mortgage companies, savings and loan associations, endowed colleges and similar sources should be contacted, since they often have properties to sell, or they might know of some client who does want to sell property. Make yourself known to their lending officials while you are there, so that you have an entree if you should later need a property loan.

Prospective sellers previously mentioned would undoubtedly be acting as principals and no real estate commission would be involved. This subject should, however, be brought up in all real estate dealings, to avoid misunderstanding on the part of buyer or seller.

Contact all real estate brokers in the area which is your hunting ground. Brokers in large communities usually specialize in certain types of properties, but it pays to contact them all anyway. A "house broker" might just have knowledge of the one commercial or other property you need for your purpose.

A direct mailing to each of the institutional sources and to all the brokers in your locale will produce results. A form letter similar to the sample shown as Exhibit 10-1 can be used. This letter was sent by our syndicate to some three hundred brokers and institutions, seeking property to buy.

EXHIBIT 10-1

SAMPLE FORM LETTER

October 6, 1969

John Jones & Son
236 South A
Big City, Large State

Gentlemen :

We have $500,000 in cash available for investment in commercial properties, preferably one-story retail stores in active areas.

We would also consider commercial property which is vacant, strategically located, and ripe for improvement.

Please furnish complete details of your offering, including photos, maps of area, lease data, financing, and price.

Prompt action will follow if we have any interest.

Yours very truly,
ALMART, INC.

By _____
                              PRESIDENT

MCH/I

Note that this Sample Form Letter, Exhibit 10-1, covers a number of important points, which are there to excite the interest of the prospective sellers or brokers to whom it is sent. These points are:

a. The amount of cash available for a deal is mentioned.
b. The type of property of interest is described.
c. An "active" commercial area is required.
d. Complete details are requested.
e. "Prompt action" is offered.
f. The indication is that a principal is inquiring.

This letter alone brought in about fifty submissions of property for sale. Two properties were bought as a result of this campaign, for a total cost of $275,000.

All submissions were inspected within two or three days, and the extent of our interest immediately conveyed to the party making the submission.

In a nutshell, it could be said that the way to obtain all possible listings for your project is to "hunt over all the ground and contact all sources for property which might be suitable and for sale."

HOW TO ACCUMULATE COMPLETE DATA

A listing has value only if it contains sufficient information to enable you to make a judgment as to your further interest in the subject property. It follows, therefore, that if this minimum information cannot be obtained, the listing should be ignored.

On the other hand, it is a waste of time to obtain complete details about property which is not suitable for your purpose, unless you have another use for this listing.

The accumulation of sufficient data to make it possible for you to decide whether you need more details requires that you equip yourself with a preliminary listing form. The form which I am thinking of is a simple one, with which to make a preliminary evaluation of a property, measured by "cash flow" generated. A printed form is not necessary; the few copies you need can be mimeographed or made on a copy machine.

The form which I prefer would be on letter-sized paper, which can be used in a three-ring binder. With this kind of form you have plenty of room to write up your notes, and a convenient place to keep them.

Exhibit 10-2 is an example of a simple preliminary listing form. Additional sheets could be prepared for more detailed information-gathering, using items taken from the checklist, Exhibit 10-3. The preliminary listing form is sufficient to give a thumbnail sketch of a property which is for sale, and enough information to enable you to decide if you need more details. Fill out this form and get the data indicated.

Most sellers, as well as brokers, are equipped with a "setup," or descriptive information about property they wish to sell. You should ask for this prior to taking piecemeal notes. The prepared information may be in the form of a descriptive statement, containing most of the information which is pertinent to the property, or it may be a brochure, complete with pictures, maps, plats and a large amount of supporting material. Ask for it and save yourself time and effort.

The information which is handed to you by the seller, or which you get piece by piece from the seller and other sources, must be studied carefully before any expressions of interest can be made.

The seller must be alerted to the fact that, while you appear to be a principal, as a representative of your syndicate you must submit offerings to your associates for consideration. This is an excellent reason for you to take along any information which can be furnished, with which to brief your partners.

Do not waste time accumulating detailed information about property which obviously is unsuitable. Do retain for your files any information you have already gathered.

EXHIBIT 10-2

PRELIMINARY LISTING FORM

Address of property _____   Type (Commercial, etc.) _____

Owner or Agent _____   Address—Phone _____

IMPROVEMENTS—General Description :   PRICE _____

_____

_____

Annual Income From Rents . . . . $_____

Less Annual Expenses . . . . $_____

Annual Net Income Before Mortgage Interest . . . . $_____

Annual Interest On Mortgage $_____ @ _____%, . $_____

Annual Net Income . . . . $_____

Less, Annual Principal Payment On Mortgage . . . . $_____

Annual Net Spendable—"Cash Flow" . . . . $_____

Land Size_____   Zoning_____   Conformity_____

Building Size_____   Construction_____

No. Units_____   Sizes of Units_____

Mortgage_____   Interest_____   Monthly Payments_____

Mortgagee_____

Tenant	Address	Monthly Rent	Lease Exp.	Percentage or rent increases

For instance, if your objective is to buy property which produces a certain return, in order to make distributions to members of your syndicate at a certain percentage rate, then a building without sufficient "cash flow" to do this is not suitable. There might be other features which offset the lack of "cash flow," such as additional unimproved land, or obvious mismanagement which can be corrected within a reasonable length of time to produce increased spendable income. Should it appear that there are logical reasons for the lack of spendable income, then it would be wise to get as much detailed information from the owner as you can, so that you can make a fair judgment of the merits of the property. Be sure to inspect any property which has even a remote chance of meeting your requirements, to give you a feel of the market and an analytical background.

Exhibit 10-3 is a detailed checklist of other items which could affect your judgment of a property, and on this list I have included many details and covered as much ground as possible. Many of the items could be extremely important to you, but to include them all on a listing form would make it entirely too cumbersome, so I suggest that you select the particulars which fit your situation. Use the checklist when you are making your analysis of offerings to make sure that you have all of the facts needed. The seller should supply most of the additional details not set out in his description of the property. Call on him for these.

Appropriate items on this same checklist can be used if vacant land or acreage is being considered to produce capital gains or deferment of earned income by means of syndication. The income from such property is usually not large, but might be sufficient to cover part of the carrying charges. Over the years this income could be an important factor which might make it possible to hold the land while awaiting a favorable market for it.

Keep all of the information which you collect, on all properties, even if you have no immediate use for the data. Facts regarding real estate rarely change rapidly, but prices and rents can change enough to revive your interest in a property which you had previously rejected as unsuitable.

A three-ring, letter-sized binder makes a good file for your listings. This should be a separate file from your listing note file. Street addresses provide a good means of identification of properties, and alphabetical filing by such addresses works well.

EXHIBIT 10-3

CHECKLIST

INCLUDES ITEMS ON PRELIMINARY LISTING FORM

1. Address of Property.

2. Owner or Agent.

3. Address and Telephone.

4. Type of Property.

5. Asking Price : Cash needed—
          Prepaid interest acceptable ?
          Installment sale acceptable ?

6. Mortgage : Original amount—   Balance to be paid ?
          Interest—   Payments—Payout at term ?
          Prepayment privileges ?
          Name of Mortgagee ?
          Address ?
          Refinancing possibilities ?

7. Land :   Size ?   Zoning ?   Conformity ?
          Covenants—Conditions—Restrictions ?
          Legal Description ?
          Easements ?
          Oil and mineral rights ?
          Access to oil and minerals ?

8. Building : Use ?   Age ?   Condition ?
          Size ?   Appearance ?
          Construction ?
          Number units ?
          Size of Units?
          Parking ?   Paved ?

9. Tenants : Names ?
          Individual rents ?
          Lease Expirations ?
          Percentages ?
          Graduated rent increases ?
          Tax participation ?
          Parking charges ?

10. Total monthly rent ?
          Other income ?

11. Total annual rent ?
          Include other income, signs, taxes, parking ?

12. Total annual expenses ?
          Taxes ?
          Repairs ?
          Parking maintenance ?
          Parking and other lighting ?
          Insurance ?
          Management ?
          Other ?

13. Net annual income before interest payment ?

14. Annual interest on mortgage ?

15. Net annual income after interest payment ?

16. Annual principal payment ?

17. Annual "cash flow" ?

18. Public improvements ?
                Sidewalks ?
                Street access ?
                Street paving ?
                Sewers ?
                Street lighting ?
                Transportation ?
                Public parking ?

19. Public Utilities ?
                Where located ?
                Gas ?
                Electricity ?
                Phone ?
                Water ?
                Rubbish removal ?

20. Taxes ?   Assessed value ?
                Assessor's market value ?
                Divide for land and building ?

21. Signs on property ?
                Sign rental ?

22. List of insurance ?

23. Leases—Check ?   Graduated increases ?   Percentage ?
                          Options ?   Tax participation ?

24. General description of property ?

25. General information ?
                Street map ?
                Pictures ?
                Residential support ?
                Tone of neighborhood ?
                Purchasing power ?
                Traffic count ?
                Blight ?
                Commercial competition ?
                Competitive square foot rents ?
                Public parking ?
                Growth influences ?

Rezoning ?
Development ?   Possible additions ?
Vacant land for development ?

When you find a property which seems to measure up to your syndicate requirements, you should go the whole way and get every bit of information which you can about the offering. The checklist, Exhibit 10-3, covers most of the items which might affect any property, and the inclusion of the checklist in your processing furnishes insurance against costly oversights.

Accumulation of complete and accurate data about property is extremely important. There is no better way to get the feel of the market and a background for valuations.

HOW TO ANALYZE THE DATA

Separate the listings which seem to fit most closely the needs and purposes of your syndicate. File them in the front of your listing book in alphabetical street order. These are the properties which stand out from the rest, and the ones on which you should focus your attention.

Separation of the few best listings should start when you begin to accumulate listings. With each new listing, you should review your thinking about which are the outstanding ones. Keep in mind that you have certain objectives for your syndicate, and that you aim to achieve them. Analysis of the data, coupled with inspection of the properties and the areas, will give you the background for making judgments of the merits of property offered.

Suppose that your syndication is to be for the purpose of producing the highest possible spendable income, to be distributed to those who join your syndicate. You might be tempted, then, to select the property with the highest net spendable income. Such property might be found to be located in a blighted area, or the improvements practically obsolete, with prospects of a short life for the high net return.

Obviously, then, "cash flow" cannot be the sole consideration in choosing a property to syndicate. You should weigh all pertinent facts, seek out opinions, and use your powers of observation prior to making judgments.

Now, how should you rate the properties so that a few stand out as your top choices?

1. Separate out the listings which are in the top third with relation to "cash flow."
2. Attach to each such listing a digest of facts and impressions which, in your opinion are the main factors which will influence your judgment.
3. Select from these listings the two or three which stand out from the rest, and make up descriptive statements or "setups" on them. See Exhibit 10-4 as an example of such a "setup."
4. Compare the advantages and disadvantages of your top two or three listings as now shown on the "setups" you have made, giving full consideration to

"cash flow" and other characteristics. Reconsider your original top third listings to make sure that you now have narrowed the field to the proper two or three. If your choice is now verified as to these few listings—that they are the ones which offer the most opportunities—reinspect these choice properties with a critical eye.

5. Compare assessed valuations of your choice two or three properties. County assessors now tend to use market value as a basis for assessment, using a reducing factor against this value. The California State Board of Equalization insists that county assessors approach 25 per cent of market value for assessment purposes. Some assessors do a remarkable job of keeping up with transfers, building costs and rents, which they use to gauge market value. Assessed valuations also show the split between land and building, a proportion valuable in figuring depreciation. Special influences and trends show up when assessed values are compared for several years back. Use this valuable tool in your analysis process.

6. Compare the loans on each of your top listings. Get an opinion (not a commitment) from one or more lending institutions, inquiring for a limit loan intended to refinance the property if that seems to be advantageous. In this way you get the advice and opinion of the appraisers of these lending institutions. They are in constant touch with the market and their opinions are valuable. Some areas may not qualify for a loan and properties in these areas should not be considered by you for syndication.

7. Keep contact with the sellers of the top third of your listings. Probe for price reductions. A price reduction or an increase in rents could raise "cash flow" and move a secondary listing into top place in your thinking.

8. Keep your comparisons going so long as listings are being accumulated, so as to keep the top listings current.

HOW TO SELECT THE ONE PROPERTY TO SYNDICATE

Your attention is now focused on one or two properties which you believe best suited for your syndication.

The background of information which you have accumulated, and the analysis which you have made, have now qualified you as a specialist, an expert with relation to this one segment of the real estate field.

Undoubtedly any one of the two or three properties which you have selected would work out well for your syndication, and there are probably several more in the top third of the listings which would also fit your requirements.

No two parcels of real estate are identical, however, and your concentrated studies must have left you with a preference. Choose the one property which you are convinced offers the best profit potential for your syndication. You have now *found the investment*.

Now, let us suppose that you have chosen 4000 Redbird Boulevard as the one property best suited for your syndicate, the one which, in your opinion, offers the greatest profit opportunities.

Exhibit 10-4, a descriptive statement, or "setup," on this property, gives most of the details which have convinced you that this is the best selection.

4000 Redbird Boulevard is a real building, and the facts about it are as stated. Only the address, name of city, and other names have been changed. The price of $175,000 is the actual purchase price of this building.

Let us analyze this property together, as you would have done with this situation.

EXHIBIT 10-4

Example of Descriptive Statement or "Setup"
(Not the true address of the building)

PRIME COMMERCIAL BUILDING

4000 REDBIRD BOULEVARD
Fandango. California.

LAND :
160 feet on Redbird Boulevard, running through to Hale Avenue, with a depth of 200 feet. Zoned C-2.

BUILDING :
Nearly new, well constructed store building, one story high, containing 8 stores, rented to six tenants. Exterior, rear and side walls of concrete blocks ; fronts of plate glass and aluminum with glass louvers above. Steel beam construction allows development of all size stores.

LOCATION :
Fandango is a city of about 50,000, in Ventura County, California. It is predicted that the county will have 1,000,000 population by 1980, with 500,000 in the Fandango area. Traffic count at this point, 30,000 cars per day on the four-lane artery. A very large new department store and two fine shopping centers are only one short block away. A large savings and loan association has just purchased the adjacent small block for a branch office.

PARKING :
Four rows of off-street parking across the entire front of the property, space for 50 cars. Deliveries on 20' strip on rear street, which is also tenant parking.

INCOME :

4000—Clipper Club	$ 425.00 to 11/30/68	
4002—Barber	125.00 to 11/30/68	
4004—Beauty shop	250.00 to 11/30/68	
4006—Auto finance	240.00 to 11/30/68	
4008-10-12—Furniture	700.00 to 11/30/68	
4016—Refrigerator repair	250.00 to 11/30/65	
TOTAL MONTHLY RENT	$1,990.00	
TOTAL ANNUAL RENTAL		$23,880.00

EXPENSES: General taxes $3,350.00
(Estimated)   Insurance, fire, liability.   500.00
               Parking lighting   200.00
               Parking sweeping   255.00
               Repairs & miscellaneous   100.00 $ 4,405.00
               NET INCOME BEFORE MORTGAGE
               REQUIREMENTS $19,475.00

TRUST DEED: First Trust Deed—Amerado, Inc., orig.
               $110,000, bal. $107,000 payable $756
               per month, 5½%, Due 9/1/83 INTEREST,
               ANNUALLY $ 5,885.00
               NET INCOME ON EQUITY—19% on
               $68,000 $13,590.00
               PAID ON PRINCIPAL, ANNUAL $ 3,187.00
               NET SPENDABLE—"Cash flow" 13.53%
               on $68,000 equity annually $10,403.00

PRICE: $175,000 Owner—Aldo, Inc. 15 W. Elm, Fandango, Calif.

---

1. The statement shows "cash flow" of 13.53 per cent on the equity, adequate to provide for contingencies and still leave a cushion for the payment of a distribution of approximately 10 per cent to those who join the syndicate. *Good!*

2. The net return, including principal paid on trust deed mortgage, shows 19 per cent on the equity. *Very Good!*

3. Expenses seem to be reasonably correct. *Satisfactory!*

4. A check of leases revealed that several leases contained options to renew for another five years, but at arbitrated rents. The furniture lease provided for a graduated increase of $50 per month at the beginning of the second year. All tenants pay their proportionate share of any tax increases. *As Represented!*

5. Building contains about 10,000 square feet. Square foot rentals average about twenty cents per square foot, per month. A check of other rents in the area indicates that this rent is low, but building operates profitably with present rents. Any breakdown in tenancy would produce a potential increase of at least 15 per cent for that space when rerented. *Good Potential!*

6. A check at city hall and county building revealed that zoning was as represented and that the building conformed to it. At the county recorder's office we found that there is an easement for utilities on the rear five feet of the land, a normal condition. Assessed values revealed that assessor had divided the assessment 60 per cent to the building and 40 per cent to the land. The valuation confirmed the tax billing. The assessor's "market value"

was low. Found that oil and mineral rights exist. *This must be worked out* in contract to purchase. Stipulate that rights be quit-claimed to depth of 500 feet and no surface entry rights, include that ten-foot side yard in Conditions, Covenants and Restrictions be eliminated.

7. A recheck at building showed that there is a roof overhang which encroaches on other property of the seller. *This must be worked out* in contract to purchase. Provide for removal of overhang, get easement for it, or deed to land below it.

8. Tenants appear to be mediocre ones. The refrigerator repair shop does not fit in with others. His lease is for one year with a four-year option. Should he go out, or any other tenant fail, more rent could be obtained when space is rerented.

All other items on the check list, those which would not be stipulated in an offer for the property, were found to be satisfactory.

OUR CONCLUSION, therefore, would be that this building measures up to our requirements, and that we should be ready to negotiate for its purchase for a real estate syndication.

POINTS TO KEEP IN MIND

√ A syndicator who is searching for an investment in real estate, to be the basis for a real estate syndication, must be equipped with forms on which to record the property listing data collected.

√ He must cover as much ground as possible to secure information about all available properties offered which are suitable for the purposes of the syndication.

√ The syndicator who hunts down all possible leads on property which meets the requirements of his contemplated syndication, develops a sense of values which is an important asset to him, and to the group which he seeks to serve.

√ The good judgment of this syndicator would then lead him to weed out all of the less desirable listings of property offered for sale, and to concentrate his attention on the one or two parcels of real estate which would be the most suitable, and potentially profitable for his contemplated real estate syndication.

CHAPTER 11—

The Time To Buy
Real Estate

Timing is extremely important to a syndicator and to the real estate syndicate which he organizes.

Proper timing with relation to engaging in any business activity, and the conducting of certain activities of the business at times which produce profit for the venture, can occur by accident, by good fortune, or by good judgment.

Good timing judgment can be acquired by gaining knowledge and experience. A real estate syndicator who has good timing judgment, and who then exercises it for the benefit of his syndicate, can do well with a deal which is properly timed by accident or good fortune, and even manage to work out a profitable deal when adverse conditions prevail. With planned good timing and favorable breaks, fantastic profits are possible.

A capable syndicator has three main activities which require proper timing in order to benefit his real estate syndicate. These activities are:

- To purchase well selected property with high profit potential, at a low price.
- To purchase the property when prices are rising.
- To refinance the property, if and when advantageous.

A syndicator must acquire a sense of timing in order to conduct these activities at a favorable time. To develop such a faculty, he must be observant and alert to the trend indicators which reflect conditions. He must develop a sense of timing so that his real estate syndicate will have the best chance of success.

The way to acquire a sense of timing

- Gain a knowledge of national conditions and events.

94

- Watch statewide developments.
- Check local trend indicators.

To gain a knowledge of national conditions, one must study the trend indicators, the reports and effects of population growth, inflation, deflation, full employment, unemployment, all-out war, part war, peace, overproduction, scarcity, tax conditions, construction, lending, total of individual incomes, family incomes, and other factors which, while national in scope, could affect local conditions.

Making a study of trend indicators is not a difficult job; in fact most businessmen are continuously making such a study. The statistics for such study appear in the newspapers, financial periodicals, trade papers and magazines. Read the papers, be alert, become informed.

Population growth is recorded by the federal census every ten years. In the interim, estimates and projections of population growth are made by others, such as public utility companies (to plan for the future), cities, (to obtain their share of federal and state taxes), school districts, politicians and others.

The results of this type of research are compiled, and the data published in almost every kind of news media, for the information of the public.

On the national scene the syndicator must be well enough grounded to make a generalized appraisal of conditions with particular attention to influences which could affect his locality and his contemplated real estate syndication.

War, peace, or in fact any national condition or situation, might exert favorable or unfavorable pressures on a locality in which a syndicator operates.

A community which has war-oriented industries as its mainstay could be hard hit if the war ended, and real estate owners would suffer. A number of cities have become stagnant because military installations have closed down. Roadside motels and other tourist attractions, which might be closed down during an all out-war, would prosper when peace comes. Timing is important to a syndicator.

A syndicator should be alert to general current market conditions and should watch for radical changes in stock averages, carloadings, metal prices, labor affairs, availability of financing, construction starts and costs, income taxes and other items of interest which might affect the timing of his venture.

The graph showing "Construction Spending" is a facsimile of such information which might be found in a financial publication or local newspaper and, when compiled from reports issued by the United States Commerce Department, such a chart would reflect a national trend which would be important to a syndicator.

Note that in the two years shown the trend is almost reversed, with the "current year" rising more rapidly at the year's end, indicating a sharp recovery in construction.

Such an upward trend in construction could be a reflection of a more plentiful supply of mortgage money, a national trend of importance to a syndicator who is determining the time to buy real estate.

Statewide developments should be watched for their local impact. The growth influences in a state are important to a syndicator when timing a deal locally. Statistics may show, for example, that the population of the country is increasing at a certain average rate.

EXHIBIT 11-1

CONSTRUCTION SPENDING

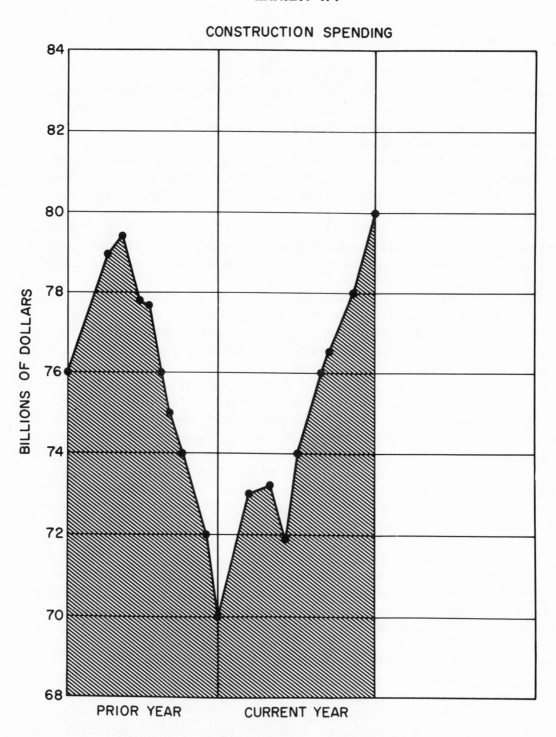

Migration within the country might increase the population of one state and lower the population of another.

A Los Angeles newspaper printed a map of California showing every county, color-keyed to a report of present county populations, coupled with a seven-year forecast of population growth by number of persons and percentage increases. Ten counties were scheduled for the largest number of new residents, 13 counties posted the largest percentage of growth, according to the report.

Ventura County, on the northwestern fringe of Los Angeles, with a forecasted 58 per cent increase, racked up the fastest pace. The population of Ventura County was given as 326,300, against a projected 517,000. Personal incomes in the county were expected to jump from a total of $737 million to $1.7 billion.

Another California county, with only a few hundred population, showed a 100 per cent increase. Such an increase would not be significant to a syndicator, because such a few people could not cause much activity in real estate.

A knowledge of national and statewide conditions is essential, as pointed out, to give a feeling of the trends which will affect local situations.

Check local conditions to coordinate this data with impressions of general conclusions about statewide and national business climate.

Local business conditions directly affect timing for any real estate syndication. Attention should be focused on local affairs when it appears that the broad outlook is favorable to engaging in a new venture in a rising market.

Local trend indicators should be thoroughly checked out by a syndicator seeking an uptrend in a local real estate market on which to launch a real estate syndication.

Local statistics can easily be obtained which disclose the trend in population growth, inflation, employment, production, construction costs, spendable income and many other pertinent facts which foretell the future of the area. The chamber of commerce, banks, utility companies, title companies, all of these furnish statistical data. Planning commissions throughout the country now have programs for master planning of cities and counties in order to participate in federal aid projects. The material which they prepare forecasts population increases, highway changes, zoning, school and public building locations, as well as prospective business expansions.

All of these sources are there to give a real estate syndicator the background for timings of his venture.

The chart entitled "Deeds Recorded in County" is a simulated graph which could be prepared from the reports issued by any county recorder.

Title companies often compile such charts, which are then usually published in the local newspapers, and an observant syndicator would look for such a significant local trend indicator.

The continuing rise in the value of deeds recorded as shown here indicates a healthy interest in real estate in this county. A rising market is one of the essential factors favoring the formation of a real estate syndicate.

A comparison of deeds recorded in one year, against comparable periods in the prior year provides valuable information to a syndicator. A rising market would encourage him to organize a real estate syndicate to get a share of the profits to be made.

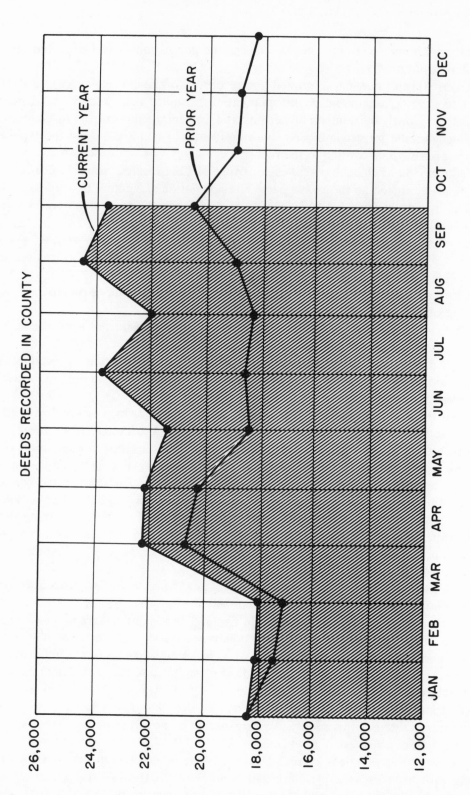

DEEDS RECORDED IN COUNTY

EXHIBIT 11-2

98

News items which are headlined, or even buried in the daily record of business and real estate transactions are a challenge to the imagination of one who is about to organize a real estate syndicate. News indicating an upward trend in values and activity stiffens his determination to activate a group ownership of real estate while the upsurge prevails.

These headlines featured news items which should fire up the interest of a real estate syndicator by forecasting the future activity in this local area:

EDISON PLANS $167 MILLION EXPANSION.

MGM BUYS 2,000 ACRES NEAR OAKS.

COUNTY GROWS 102 PER DAY.

20-YEAR POPULATION EXPLOSION.

KAISER WILL BUILD $5.5 MILLION PLANT.

SEVEN-ACRE HIGHWAY TRACT SOLD FOR $244,000.

The community referred to has a population of about 65,000. It boasts of a new $7 million department store complex, a $1 million medical instrument plant, a multimillion dollar plastic manufacturing facility, a yacht harbor for over 500 pleasure craft—all new developments. There is a deep-water harbor ready for expansion.

These trend indicators are evidence that the future of the area is bright, and that a general upsurge of values will be felt and growth will continue.

An analysis of the headlines immediately shows the indicators which are most positive. The Edison expansion to triple the production of electricity within four years is the most outstanding. These new plants will pay over $4 million in real estate taxes annually. Construction and staffing will bring salaries of $500,000 for the next four years. The investment of $167 million is based on company confidence that electricity use will increase dramatically.

The manufacturing plants, new to the area, are going to spend outside money for construction and employ local labor when built.

MGM will spend millions on moving picture production facilities, and their employees will probably inject an entirely new type of buying group with high purchasing power into the area.

The population growth and projections are impressive, but the trend could change. The land purchases could just be speculation. These are fine indicators, but not so solid as the others. Timing, however, takes into consideration all factors and influences which the indicators show as a trend. When the trend is up, the indicators usually all point in the same direction.

Thus, as would be expected, there are few residential vacancies in this area, almost no stores for rent, and the resale of pre-used houses is going well. The number of unsold new houses has been cut in half in the past year. Subdivision and residential building is moderate in quantity, but increasing. This community is on the verge of an upsurge and the timing would be right here for a real estate syndicator to activate a venture.

Large land and research companies advertise with fancy brochures by direct mail in an endeavor to interest prospects in land speculation.

One of these companies sent me a handsome brochure detailing the advantages of land investment in the area east of Los Angeles. Included with a glowing description of the future of the area, there was a graph similar to the one shown as Exhibit 11-3.

The curve shown on this graph represents the phases of evolution from dormant, unused land to the point at which redevelopment is required.

This type of graph is usually plotted from some statistical data which must be averaged to get the starting point in the "dormant phase," and for this reason no figures are given in dollar values. I arbitrarily inserted the five-year intervals shown on the graph, and while most land development companies advocate the purchase of land in what they call the "maximum yield" and "dynamic phase," I recommend purchase of land in the "development phase," because it appears that values will double within a five-year period in this phase.

Anyone can make a graph like this by plotting assessed values of a number of parcels of land, then averaging out the curve and continuing the upward sweep of an optimistic projection of increased values.

Pictorial material such as this graph can make an impression on people who might invest in land, or join in a syndicate for the purpose of acquiring land in order to benefit by an appreciation in value over a short period.

Land research firms claim that large profits can be made by purchasing land in the path of development and then waiting for a rise in land prices.

Studies made by a land research firm presumably make it possible for them to select the areas of most rapid growth, and to predict the timing which would bring the biggest profits for an investor.

There is no doubt that land research can make a valuable contribution to a venture which involves the purchase of acreage or vacant land for capital appreciation, as well as to convert high earned income of investors into long-term capital gain, possibly in another year when the investors are in a lower bracket.

The research is done to locate pressure areas so that land can be bought at a time when prices are about to be forced up. Good research should result in good timing.

A syndicator who intends to operate in acreage or vacant land would do well to become a land researcher himself before engaging in a venture. Then individual properties could be charted, with actual values used, to plot a curve which should help in timing a deal for a real state syndication. Success depends on good timing.

Timing for the syndication of improved real estate must encompass not only the general business climate, but must include a study of the neighborhood in which the property is located, the future prospects of the subject property, and the conditions which confront the seller.

General business conditions were relatively good when negotiations were being conducted for the purchase of the property 4000 Redbird Boulevard.

The property had been on the market for some time because the seller wanted to enter into another venture. The size of the equity was undoubtedly an obstacle to a ready sale of the property. Buyers want more "leverage." The mortgage was small with prepayment

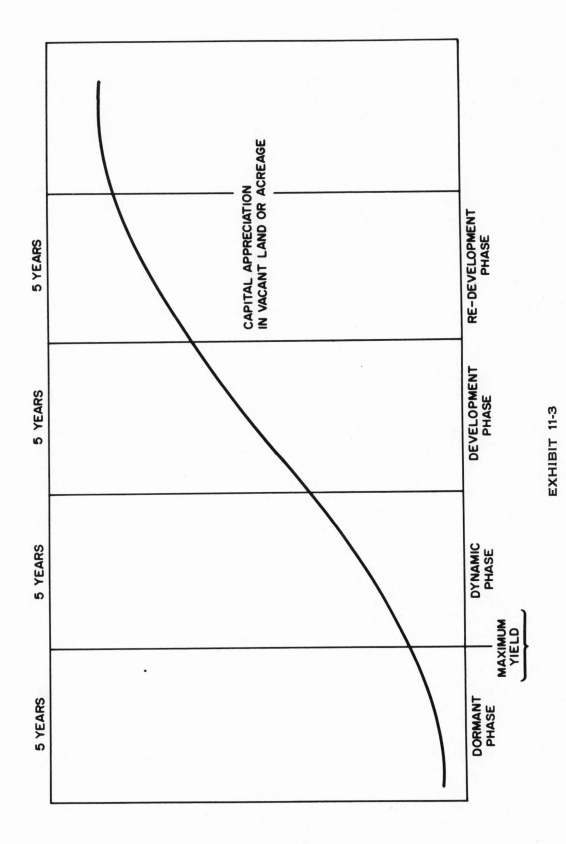

EXHIBIT 11-3

101

penalties, which made it impractical to refinance such a low-interest mortgage in a tight money market. The seller would not consider taking back secondary financing himself. These are the conditions which faced the seller and made him open to a consideration of a much lower purchase price. This would be a good time for a buyer to negotiate for the purchase of the property.

An estimate of the rents which might be expected in the next few years seemed to be in order, and such a projection was made by comparing rents in the area, and plotting the capitalized value of the building at the rents expected, showing the asking price, the average price which buyers might pay, and the price which was later the negotiated price. See Exhibit 11-4.

The chart shows a moderate rent increase to be expected over a period of the next four years, and I have plotted it as it actually happened for the first two years and ten months.

Increased net income was anticipated primarily because one lease was expiring, and rent could be raised. Another lease had a provision for increased rent in the second year. The balance of the increase was due to a tenant failure. This space was rerented to a new, responsible tenant, at a higher rental against percentage of sales.

The charting of the performance of the 4000 Redbird Boulevard property could be done by anyone who analyzed the leases, inspected the property and checked rents in the area.

A projection of the findings, plotted on the graph, could not fail to reveal that there was an excellent chance for a reasonable increase in net rents during the next four years after acquisition of the property, and a real opportunity for a spectacular rise in net income when the bulk of the leases expired at the end of four years.

The time seemed to be the right one to buy this real estate. The owner was anxious to sell, and soft on his price. The property, improved with a new building, had a good earning record, satisfactory for syndication, with prospects of an immediate increase in the net income. Most of the leases would expire at the end of four years, and at that time a spectacular raise in net income could be expected if rents were increased to prevailing rates. *The time for buying this property was right!*

The area in which the property is located was at that time well developed, with successful stores and shopping facilities, with room for further improvements. There were no stores available for rent except the one about to be vacated in the subject building. *The timing for the area was right!*

The city in which this shopping area is located was rapidly developing. Trend indicators pointed to an explosion of population and business. *The timing for the city was right!*

The state was experiencing a tremendous growth, looking forward to becoming the most populous state in the country. *The timing for the state was right!*

Nationally, prices were rising, with no breakdowns in sight at the time. *Nationally, the time was right!*

An example such as this one shows how the trend indicators can be used to determine the time to buy real estate.

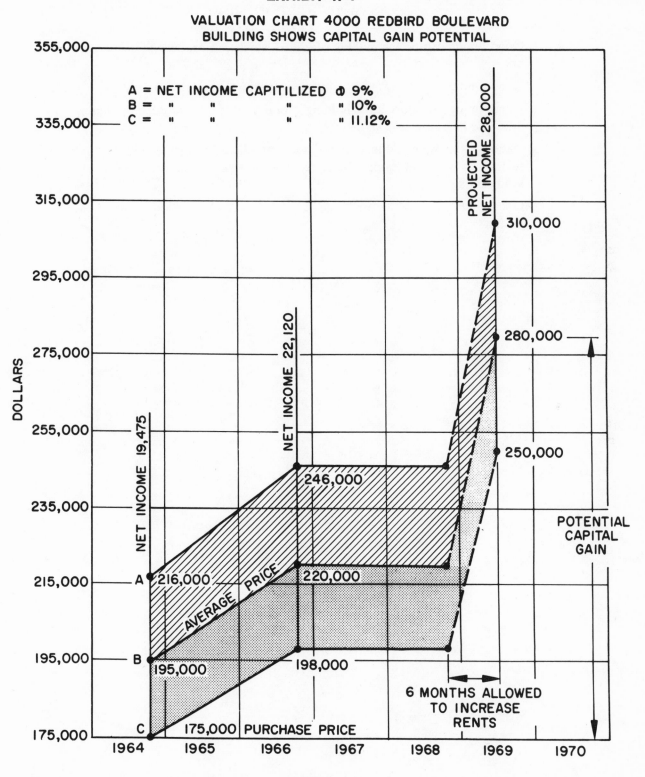

EXHIBIT 11-4

VALUATION CHART 4000 REDBIRD BOULEVARD
BUILDING SHOWS CAPITAL GAIN POTENTIAL

A = NET INCOME CAPITILIZED @ 9%
B = " " " " 10%
C = " " " " 11.12%

DOLLARS

NET INCOME 19,475

NET INCOME 22,120

PROJECTED NET INCOME 28,000

310,000

280,000

250,000

246,000

216,000 A

220,000

195,000 B

198,000

175,000 PURCHASE PRICE C

AVERAGE PRICE

POTENTIAL CAPITAL GAIN

6 MONTHS ALLOWED TO INCREASE RENTS

1964   1965   1966   1967   1968   1969   1970

103

POINTS TO KEEP IN MIND

√ Good timing can be the making of a deal which can produce fantastic profits.

√ Good timing eliminates most of the risks from a real estate syndication.

√ Good timing can shorten the holding period needed to conclude a profitable syndicated real estate deal.

√ National, statewide and local trend indicators should be included in the considerations of a syndicator who is seeking the right timing for a real estate syndication.

√ Good timing judgment can be acquired by alert observation of trend indicators.

CHAPTER 12—

Negotiating the Purchase

Syndicators John J. Jones and Samuel S. Smith, having decided that the time is right for forming a real estate syndicate, and having selected 4000 Redbird Boulevard as the property, decided to negotiate for the purchase of it.

Negotiating means coming to terms, so that buyer and seller have a meeting of minds. The negotiations must lead to an option to purchase or a contract to purchase the property, so that the syndicators control the property prior to forming a real estate syndicate.

This chapter points out a way to control a property by negotiation and contract.

ASSUMPTIONS

1. That the asking price of the 4000 Redbird Boulevard property was higher than the negotiated purchase price of $175,000, which was the contract price.
2. That John J. Jones, partner of Samuel S. Smith, will be the negotiator, together with the broker representing the seller.
3. The listed price of the property is $216,000, based on the net income capitalized at a 9 per cent return on the building clear of encumbrance.

THE PURCHASE CAN BE NEGOTIATED THIS WAY

- Brief the negotiators.
- List merits and demerits of the property.
- Prepare an option to purchase.
- Prepare a purchase contract (leave out purchase price).
- Get seller's approval of contract terms, other than price.
- Negotiate the purchase price.
- Get a signed option to purchase, or a contract to purchase the property at the negotiated price.

The aim of this method of negotiating the purchase is to get the seller to agree to a deal which allows the syndicators time to work out their syndication. The seller must be sold on the idea that it takes time to put a real estate syndicate together and that such a group can be induced to join only in a deal which is firmly committed. Once the seller agrees to the terms of the contract to purchase, then the price is arrived at and the contract is signed.

One advocate of this method of negotiating the purchase put it this way: "Negotiating the price first puts the seller in a strong position. He feels that he now has his price, and becomes obstinate about unimportant contract provisions which pose problems for a syndicator. Leave the contract price negotiation until the last and then it is easy to get the contract signed."

SEVEN STEPS NEGOTIATE THE PURCHASE

Brief the negotiators

We have assumed that our negotiators will be one of the syndicators, John J. Jones, who will work with the cooperating broker who represents the seller.

Jones and Smith know the procedure which will be used, and they brief the cooperating broker. Together they prepare the documents which will be used, and review the arguments which should persuade the seller to agree to the terms of the contract and then to agree to an acceptable purchase price. This document, option or purchase contract, will, when signed, control the property and allow time to form the real estate syndicate.

List merits and demerits of subject property

Listing these features gives the negotiator arguments to persuade the seller to agree to terms of the purchase contract, and, when terms are agreeable, to work out a purchase price.

A sophisticated negotiator will not dwell on the undesirable features of a property to the exclusion of obvious qualities.

Using the 4000 Redbird Boulevard building as an illustration, these would be some of the points.

Undesirable features:

    a. The land is under-improved. Although zoned C-2, which would allow a six-story improvement, the building is one story high, with 10,000 square feet rentable.
    b. The architecture is not appealing.
    c. The color of the building is not attractive.
    d. The tenants are local merchants with little financial strength.
    e. The rents are too low.
    f. Leases, except one, are for four more years.
    g. The mortgage is too small; little "leverage."
    h. Penalties for pre-payment of mortgage preclude financing.

i. The block is undeveloped except for one other small shoe store building.

k. The marquee projects four feet out on each side of the building, leaving an awkward, unusable strip of land on each side for which taxes must be paid.

l. One tenant conducts a beer bar business. Parking lights are required until 2 A.M. each day. This costs money for electricity. Beer bars pose management problems.

Desirable features:

a. The building is only one year old.

b. There is customer parking adequate for the conduct of the business of the tenants, and space in the rear for tenant parking and deliveries.

c. Other commercial improvements in the neighborhood are relatively new and occupied by successful tenants.

d. The largest parcel of vacant land in the shopping area, consisting of about ten acres, has a sign on it which states that a large discount department store is to be built on the site.

e. The building is set back from the street, but is visible from both directions, furnishing good advertising for the tenants.

f. The interest rate on the loan is at $5\frac{1}{2}$ per cent; the loan was a twenty-year term first trust deed, with nineteen years to go until maturity. Monthly payments of $756.68 will pay the loan out fully at maturity.

The negotiators are to use the observations listed to persuade the seller to agree to the terms of the purchase agreement or option presented, provided that a purchase price can thereafter be agreed upon.

A few of the obvious advantages which the property has on the credit side can be pointed out to soften up the recitation of the disadvantages or demerits with which the seller is undoubtedly familiar. These persuasive arguments have some value, but the main interest of this seller is to get cash for his equity, so that he can get into another deal. This is the clincher, to be held back until the other terms of the contract or option are agreed upon.

Prepare an option to purchase

The preparation of an option to purchase the property could be done because it is a simple way to get control of the property on terms which the syndicator can use to get the deal nailed down, subject to determination of the purchase price, and to provide time to work out the syndication.

An option is a contract by which a landowner gives to another party (the optionee) the right to buy the property at a fixed price and on certain agreed terms within a specified period of time. The optionee gets the right to call for and receive the property if he chooses, and if he complies with the terms of the option agreement within the specified time. The optionee usually pays for the option, and he cannot recover the money paid if he lets the time go by without exercising his option. The option, if exercised, is usually superceded by a contract to purchase the property.

Some optionees get an option for the express purpose of using it as a base for further negotiations of price and terms. Most sellers feel that an option is a one-sided document, with the optionee having all the choices, getting control of the seller's property with almost no cash outlay.

An option could be tried out, and if not acceptable to a seller, then a contract to purchase could be substituted. I try to insert some of the features of an option to purchase in a contract to purchase, making a sort of combination of the two. Once a straight option agreement has been presented, however, this is hard to get over to the seller.

An option to purchase property should be prepared by competent legal counsel, fully cognizant of local law. The purchase price should be left out for later negotiation.

Preparing a contract to purchase

The contract to purchase real estate which a syndicator would use is actually an option to purchase, but the option is incorporated in the contract.

This contract to purchase, or option, is the key to successful real estate syndication, and anyone who wants to be a syndicator must realize this. It is absolutely essential that the syndicator should have control of the real estate to be syndicated, on the best terms obtainable, at the lowest possible price, and for a period long enough to work out his deal.

There is some financial risk in getting control of property by contract to purchase or option. All or part of the cash deposit may be forfeited if the syndicator fails to raise the cash required to close the deal. A syndicator who has properly laid the groundwork, however, knows that he can raise enough capital to consummate his deal.

A contract to purchase real estate can be drawn for a specific type of deal, and such a contract deserves to be seriously considered. One syndicator, who works on acreage, uses a contract to purchase which provides that a promissory note is the deposit; he then assumes existing encumbrances and offers another promissory note for the balance of the purchase price. I believe that I would have a hard time finding a seller who would entertain such an offer.

Major oil companies do get options to purchase valuable corners for periods up to ninety days with considerations of $10 to $20 as payment for the option. Sellers make these options because they know that these large companies have the problem of checking out the property for their use, and of getting company approval of the site selections made by field workers in their land acquisition departments.

Oil companies usually option property at the seller's asking price, with the thought that they can continue negotiations about the price during the term of the option. Thus, the option is obtained with minimum resistance, since the company which is to be the buyer is large and able to pay cash, and appears to be offering the full asking price.

The contract to purchase, which I have included as Exhibit 12-1, covers a number of points which would be important to a syndicator, and purports to be an offer to purchase the property at 4000 Redbird Boulevard.

This illustration is not intended to be a model. An important document such as a contract to purchase real estate or an option to purchase should be prepared by competent legal counsel.

EXHIBIT 12-1

STANDARD PURCHASE AGREEMENT

and DEPOSIT RECEIPT

_____ California, _____ 19____ RECEIVED FROM _____, herein called the Buyer, the sum of Five Thousand and No/100 Dollars ($5,000.00), evidenced by Cashier's check, made payable to _____ Title Insurance Company, (_____ Branch), as deposit on account of the purchase price of _____ ($_____) for the purchase of property located in the City of Fandango, County of Ventura, California, described as follows: Parcel No. 2 in Block I, Ocean Tract, as per map recorded in Book _____, Page _____, of Maps, in the office of the Recorder of said Ventura County, being on the east side of Redbird Boulevard, with frontage of 160.0 feet, and with a depth on both north and south lot lines of 200.0 feet to Hale Avenue, on which the lot frontage is 160.0 feet. Improvements consist of a one-story concrete block commercial building containing approximately 10,000 square feet of floor area, divided into eight retail stores. The property is commonly known as 4000–4016 Redbird Boulevard.

The purchase price of $_____ is to be payable as follows:

Buyer shall pay the sum of $_____ in cash into an escrow to be opened with the above-named Title Insurance Company, including the deposit made herewith; one hundred and twenty days shall be allowed the Buyer and Seller to close escrow. The Buyer shall take title subject to the existing First Trust Deed described below, which has an unpaid principal balance of approximately $107,000.

If Buyer fails to pay the balance of said purchase price, or to complete said purchase as herein provided, the sum of $1,000.00 may be retained by Seller at his option as consideration for the execution of this agreement by Seller.

Title is to be free of liens and encumbrances other than those set forth herein. Title subject to General and Special Taxes for fiscal year 1964–65, to conditions, covenants, restrictions and easements, reservations, rights, rights of way, and the exception of water on or under said land, now of record, and the exception of the mineral, petroleum, oil, natural gases and hydrocarbon substances underlying said land, as granted to _____ Construction Company in Deed recorded _____ 1952, as Document No. _____, in Book _____, Page _____, of official Records, providing same contains no right of surface entry. Mortgage or Trust Deed securing an indebtedness as per its terms, now of record (Lender's statement to show an unpaid balance of principal of $107,000, but if same should show to be more or less than said amount, then the total consideration is to be kept the same as shown above, by accordingly adjusting the cash through escrow.)

Evidence of title shall be a California Land Title Association standard coverage form policy of title insurance issued through _____ Title Insurance Company, to be paid for by _____. If Seller is unable to convey a marketable title, except as herein provided, within three months after acceptance hereof by Seller, or if the improvements of said property be destroyed or materially damaged prior to transfer of title, then upon the demand of Buyer, said deposit and all other sums paid by Buyer shall be returned to Buyer, and this agreement as between Buyer and Seller shall be of no further effect, and Seller shall become obligated to pay all expenses incurred in connection with examination of title.

Taxes, premiums on insurance acceptable to Buyer, rents, interest and other expenses of said property shall be prorated as of the date of transfer of title. The amount of any bond or assessment which is a lien shall be paid by _____, except that the amount of any delinquency now existing shall be paid by Seller. Seller shall pay the cost of revenue stamps on deed and any expense connected with removal of title defects.

Possession of said property to be delivered to Buyer on closing escrow.

This offer shall be deemed revoked unless accepted in writing within _____ days after date hereof, and such acceptance is communicated to Buyer within said period.

Seller represents:

1. That the property is Zoned C-2, and that the improvement thereon conforms to the zoning.
2. That the Seller will furnish, at his expense, a survey to be made by a State Licensed Surveyor showing the building within the lot lines and with all corners of the lot identified by markers.
3. That the Seller will furnish a set of plans and specifications of the existing structure.
4. That each store space is equipped with a suspended gas-fired space heater and a gas-fired hot water heater, further that this equipment is the property of the Seller, that the Seller will include this equipment as part of the property to be conveyed, and that the Buyer will be furnished with a Bill of Sale conveying said equipment to Buyer.
5. That the existing First Trust Deed, originally for a 20-year term, in the original principal amount of $110,000.00, with present unpaid balance of approximately $107,000.00, is due 9/1/1983, with monthly payments of $756.68, including interest at $5\frac{1}{2}\%$, that the lender is Amerado, Inc., and that the Trust Deed does not provide that the lender can demand pre-payment of the principal amount of the loan if the property is sold to another owner. A Buyer can therefore take title subject to the existing loan.
6. Seller will provide a list of tenants, leases, rents, lease expirations and lease guarantee deposits. Seller agrees to exhibit said leases to Buyer, and further agrees that this contract is subject to the approval of said leases by Buyer.
7. Lease guarantees which have been deposited with Seller by tenants, in the total sum of $2,040.00, shall be credited to Buyer at close of escrow.

Buyer represents:

1. That the Buyer, Samuel S. Smith, is acting for a Limited Partnership to be formed for the acquisition of the subject property, further that he will be one of the General Partners of said Limited Partnership, and that John J. Jones, who is also acting as a real estate broker in this transaction, will be the other General Partner.
2. That the Buyer reserves the right to assign his interest in this purchase contract to said Limited Partnership or to any other person or organization, for a consideration which will not be disclosed.

EXHIBIT 12-1 (CONTINUED)

3. That the Buyer assumes no personal liability for the consummation of this transaction, and that all obligations to the Seller shall be considered to have been met by the forfeiture of the sum of $1,000.00 as provided for herein, in the event that the Buyer shall fail to provide funds to complete the transaction.

Time is of the essence of this contract, but the Broker may, without notice, extend for a period not to exceed one month the time for performance of any act hereunder, except the time for the acceptance hereof by Seller and the date of possession.

_____   _____
Real Estate Broker   By

_____   _____
Address   Telephone

The undersigned Buyer offers and agrees to buy the above described property on the terms and conditions above stated and acknowledges receipt of a copy hereof.

_____   _____
Buyer   Address

_____   _____
City   Telephone

Buyer to take title in the name of _____

_____.

ACCEPTANCE

We, the undersigned, do accept the above offer and agree to sell the property described herein on the terms and conditions as set forth herein.

We further agree to pay Broker or Brokers herein named and employed by the undersigned to sell said property as commission the sum of _____

_____ ($_____), which sum is to be divided equally between said Brokers.

The undersigned acknowledges receipt of a copy of this contract.

Dated _____ 19_____.

_____
                Seller

_____   _____
Telephone   Address and City

EXHIBIT 12-1 (CONTINUED)

Exhibit 12-1, the so-called Standard Purchase Agreement, is the syndicator's won standard agreement. It is a framework which the syndicator uses to tie up the property for a period of time which enables him to raise the money to close the deal, and contains provisions which are satisfactory to the syndicator.

1. The deposit of $5,000 is made payable to the escrow agent.
2. There is a provision for a forfeit of only $1,000 in the event that the syndicator cannot raise money enough to close escrow.
3. The time to close escrow is 120 days, to give the syndicator time to get his group to put up the cash to close the deal.
4. The seller has been put on notice that the buyer is acting for a purchasing group, of which he is to be one of the general partners, and one of the brokers is to be the other general partner.
5. The buyer has reserved the right to assign the contract to purchase without disclosing the consideration to be paid for the assignment thereof.
6. The purchase price is to be inserted after terms of the contract to purchase are agreed to by seller.

Much depends on the skill with which the negotiators present their arguments. In the case of the 4000 Redbird Boulevard property they could point to the large equity, expense of refinancing, mediocre financial status of the tenants, under-improvement of the land, and, with due caution, to the unattractive appearance of the improvement. The negotiators must intersperse these arguments with admissions of some of the attractive features of the property to avoid offending the seller.

In the 4000 Redbird Boulevard transaction, the seller was persuaded that it was to his advantage to sell at a price which was slightly lower than the average for such a parcel, because the financing was inadequate and the equity therefore very large, proportionately. A contract offer to purchase at a price of $175,000 was accepted by the seller because there were few buyers who would invest such a large amount in the equity, and the seller needed cash for another deal.

POINTS TO KEEP IN MIND

√ A syndicator who is about to negotiate a deal to control property suitable for a contemplated real estate syndication should assemble all facts and arguments which might persuade the seller to commit himself to sell on the terms required by the syndicator/buyer.

√ The principal requirements of the syndicator/buyer are these:
   a. That the seller should tie up the property for a long enough period so that the syndicator/buyer can organize his group and raise the money to complete the transaction.
   b. That the option or contract to purchase the property shall give control of the deal to the syndicator/buyer at the least possible cost to him if he, as the purchaser, fails to perform within the time agreed upon.

   c. That the price to be paid for the property shall be mutually agreed upon *after* the seller has agreed to the other terms of the offer.

√ The negotiator for the syndicator/buyer should be equipped with all of the persuasive arguments with which to convince the seller to enter into an agreement to sell the property on the syndicator/buyer's terms.

√ The negotiator for the syndicator/buyer should have with him the documents, which will commit the seller to tie up the property when he executes them.

CHAPTER 13—

Management of the
Syndicate

The business affairs of the syndicate require management as distinguished from the management of the syndicate real estate.

The syndicators are the managers of syndicate affairs, and as such they are charged with the duties which would be assumed by the officers or directors of any business organization, or by individuals who are owners of real estate.

The syndicate investors, the inactive participants, are entitled to have the affairs of the syndicate efficiently managed. The syndicators are to be compensated for the express purpose of relieving the investors of any management problems.

ORGANIZATIONAL MANAGEMENT

Management of the affairs of a real estate syndicate begins even before it is organized. The syndicators decide on the type of real estate to syndicate, look into the factors which are favorable to forming a real estate syndicate, lay the groundwork, form a preliminary organization, settle on the qualifications and scope of work of professionals to be employed, find, attract and convince investors. The syndicators also determine the type of business organization to use, find the investment, study timing and negotiate the purchase of the property. All of these items are a part of management of a real estate syndicate.

OPERATIONAL MANAGEMENT

When property is purchased and the syndicate holds title to the real estate, there are operational management duties which are the responsibilities of the syndicators.

Some syndicators are also real estate managers, and they manage the real estate for the syndicate, as in the case of the 4000 Redbird Boulevard deal. In this instance one of the syndicators, a property manager, undertook the management of syndicate property for a customary management fee. Other syndicators employ property managers who have no financial interest in the real estate syndicate. Professional management of syndicate real estate is covered in Chapter 14. The syndicators should direct the professional property manager with respect to policy matters and major expenditures for maintenance and remodeling.

The share which syndicators take in the management of syndicate real estate depends to a great extent on the type of real estate owned.

A syndicate which owns acreage or vacant land has few management problems. The management job consists of payment of taxes and interest, keeping check on neighborhood developments as to comparative land prices, watching local conditions, and maintenance of the few improvements, fences, signs, etc. A land syndicator would undertake this type of real estate management as part of the management of syndicate affairs. The syndicator would also see to the preparation of syndicate tax returns and keep the investors informed. See Chapter 15, "Reports to Investors."

Other management of syndicate land is covered in subsequent chapters, such as Chapter 16, "How to Increase the Value of Property."

The syndicator who manages unimproved land should not fail to get compensation for his services as manager of the syndicate real estate. The simplicity of the job tempts one to manage the property without charge, but a syndicator should always make a fair charge for out-of-pocket expenses and time expended. One land syndicator of my acquaintance found this out when he syndicated a number of parcels of land. He now charges 5 per cent of the purchase price of the land for handling the detail work.

The ownership of improved property by a real estate syndicate presents an entirely different management situation for a syndicator.

There is income from the property. The manager of the real estate should be supervised; a syndicate bank account should be established and accounted for; tax returns need to be prepared; reports and distributions must be made to investors; the syndicator is in fact concerned with all of the activities covered in the subsequent chapters of this book as related to the syndicate property.

Every activity which an individual property owner would engage in, and every responsibility which such an owner would be charged with, should be a part of the management program of a syndicator.

Scope of operational management

As an example of the scope of the management responsibility of a real estate syndicator, I point out that the real estate tax is the largest single item of expense in the operation of real estate, and that a syndicator should do everything which is possible to minimize this expense. Every dollar of tax money saved adds to the net income from the property!

Assessed valuations should be checked by the owners of all real estate, and syndicators should be alert to work on any situation which will hold the valuations down.

In a neighboring city the city fathers decided to pass legislation requiring that the owners provide off-street parking. Protests were of no avail, and the parking law was put into effect.

As part owner of a parcel of vacant commercial land, I felt that the value was less with the parking requirement, and yet, of course, one way or another automobile parking must be provided to attract customers.

The county assessor's office, however, thought that this land was due for a large increase in assessed valuation, but we were able to convince the assessor that the parking requirement had offset the increase, due to the restricted use of the land. The result was that there was no increase in the taxes, lower carrying charges for the vacant parcel, and lower expenses for an improved parcel which we owned.

A real estate manager could not be expected to handle a matter of this kind; he is not paid to do it. This type of activity is the responsibility of an owner of property, and it would be the job of a syndicator when a real estate syndicate owns the property.

In addition to other activities as outlined in this book, the syndicators have these managerial responsibilities:

- Manage the syndicate bank account
- Make a projected rent schedule (for income property)
- Project the capital gain potential
- Determine property management policy
- Analyze the real estate
- Determine depreciation schedule
- Consider refinancing
- Make distributions to investors

Managing the syndicate bank account

In order to do this efficiently, the bank account should be a separate account used strictly for the conduct of the business of the real estate syndicate.

The bank account should be in the name of the syndicate organization, preferably with two signatures required on checks. The account can be arranged so that limited amounts for payment of small obligations could be checked out with only one signature, for convenience.

The bank in which the account is to be kept should be conveniently located, but that should not be the primary objective. Consideration should be given to the financial assistance which might be rendered to the syndicate by the bank which is chosen as a depository. There are times when it is found to have been well worth while to travel a little farther to deal with a larger or more accommodating banking institution.

A syndicator should provide for raising enough money so that there will be a reasonable amount of working capital in the syndicate bank account. This makes it possible to pay the occasional large bills, such as the real estate tax bill, without requiring the collection of emergency assessments from the investors.

A syndicator whose operation is in vacant land would use this account for the purpose of accumulating the assessments to be paid by the syndicate investors for the purpose of paying real estate taxes, interest, insurance, management and miscellaneous expenses.

A land syndicator should anticipate and schedule the assessments which the investors are expected to pay to operate the real estate, so that the working surplus is not depleted. It is the duty of the syndicator to see to the collection of the assessments when they are due.

The real estate syndicate which owns income property uses the syndicate bank account as the depository for net rentals received from the managing agent at the end of each month.

The syndicators usually make mortgage payments and pay for major maintenance expenditures, and also for capital items such as remodeling, all such payments being made out of the syndicate account.

Cash distributions to investors should be paid out of the syndicate bank account, as well as the share of distributions paid to the syndicators, usually at the end of the fiscal or calendar year.

The Redbird Boulevard syndicate had a real estate manager as one of the syndicators, and he was to manage the property. This is not always the case, however, and when a managing agent is not financially interested in the real estate syndicate, it is well to separate the day-to-day management of the property from the dealings which are the confidential business of the members of the syndicate group.

The syndicators should budget the expenditures of the syndicate against expected income in order to adjust payment of distributions to investors if that becomes necessary to pay the bills of the business.

Making a projected rent schedule (for income property)

A projected rent schedule, which forecasts the rents that appear to be obtainable within the forseeable future, is an important tool of the syndicators. Exhibit 13-1 is an example of such a projection of expected rental income from the 4000 Redbird Boulevard property.

The exhibit shows the rents as they were when the building was acquired, as they were one year later and two years later. The right-hand column shows the rent schedule as anticipated when the leases on six stores expire. The new rentals would be effective at the end of four years of operation of the property.

Of the increases which show up at the beginning of the second year of operations, the increase in the rent of the furniture tenant was provided for in the lease, while the raise to $500 for the Clipper Club was due to a tenant breakdown. The lease to the store at 4016 Redbird expired and the space was rerented at the higher rent shown, for a short term, with valuable remodeling done at the expense of the tenant.

As of 12/1/66: The increase in rents in this year was due to the expiration of the savings and loan short lease. Another short lease was made with this tenant at $350 per month. The new lease was made with 30¢ per square foot per month as the basis, this being the prevailing rate for similar store space in the area. The previous short lease with this tenant had been made at a lower rate because of the remodeling done at tenant expense. At this time 30¢ per square foot per month was considered to be a fair rent for all the stores, but most of them had long leases at lower rents.

As of 12/1/68: The right-hand column of the rent projection schedule, under this date, shows all store rentals as anticipated rentals with the exception of the Clipper Club, for which a longer lease had been made. The savings and loan was expected to go out during this year, into its own building.

Anticipated rentals are projected on the basis of 30¢ per square foot per month, because several leases have options for extensions at negotiated rentals, and the 30¢ rate has been established, and could be shown as the prevailing rent, unless changed by later developments.

The syndicate managers should keep in close touch with the rental market as the time approaches for the renewal of these leases.

EXHIBIT 13-1

4000 REDBIRD BOULEVARD PROPERTY

Projection of Rents

Address Tenant		Rent 11/30/64	Rent 12/1/65	Rent 12/1/66	New Rent Schedule 12/1/68
4000	"Clipper" Club	$425			
	"Clipper" new		$500*	500 to 11/30/73	$500 to 11/30/73 + %
4002	Barber	125	125	125 to 11/30/68	200 Anticipated
4004	Beauty Shop	250	250	250 to 11/30/68	350 "
4006	Auto Finance	240	240	240 to 11/30/68	300 "
4008	Furniture	700	750**	750 to 11/30/68	350 "
4010	"				350 "
4012	"				350 "
4016	Refrig. Rep.	250			
	Sav. & Loan		300***	350	350 "
Monthly rents		$1,990	$2,165	$2,215	$2,750
Annual rents		$23,880	$25,980	$26,580	$33,000

*New tenant
**Rent increase provided in lease
***New tenant

The graph, Exhibit 13-2, "Projection of Rents," was plotted from the data on Exhibit 13-1 as shown on line A.

Line B shows the estimated expenses of operating the building, including real estate taxes. Expense was estimated at approximately $4,000 per annum until December 1,

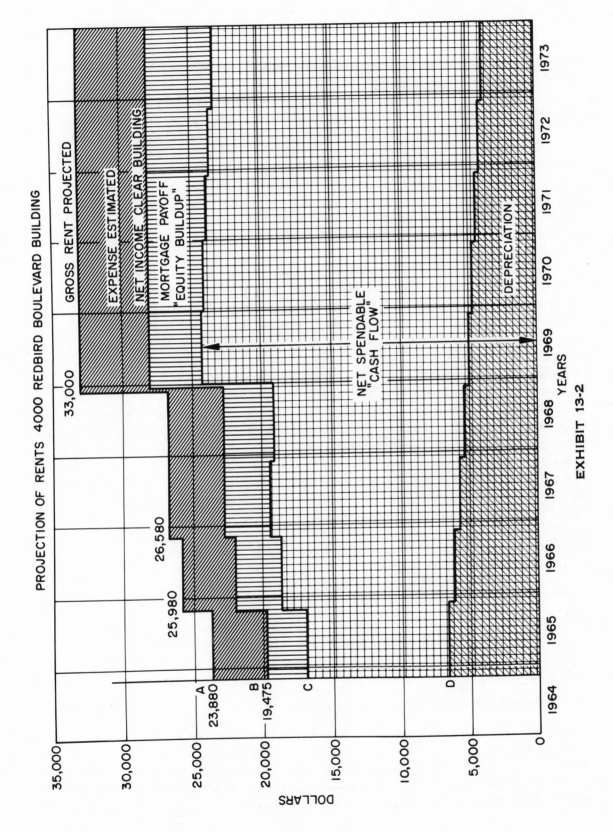

PROJECTION OF RENTS 4000 REDBIRD BOULEVARD BUILDING

GROSS RENT PROJECTED

EXPENSE ESTIMATED

NET INCOME CLEAR BUILDING

MORTGAGE PAYOFF "EQUITY BUILDUP"

NET SPENDABLE "CASH FLOW"

DEPRECIATION

33,000

26,580

25,980

A 23,880

B 19,475

C

D

DOLLARS

35,000

30,000

25,000

20,000

15,000

10,000

5,000

0

1964 1965 1966 1967 1968 1969 1970 1971 1972 1973

YEARS

EXHIBIT 13-2

1968, at which time the estimate was increased to $5,000 per annum. Leases provide for tenants paying increases in real estate taxes, which accounts for the steady rate of expense.

Line C on the graph shows the mortgage payoff or equity buildup, which increases from approximately $3,000 in the first year of operation to over $4,000 in the ninth year. The increased equity buildup reduces the "cash flow" at an increasing rate as the mortgage matures. The syndicate managers should be alert to this feature of the financing, and at an appropriate time consider refinancing the property.

Line D on the graph shows the depreciation scheduled for the 4000 Redbird Boulevard Building as it declines over the nine-year period.

The syndicate owners of the 4000 Redbird building would not be the "first users," so that accelerated depreciation could not be considered, even if available by Internal Revenue Service regulations.

A building valuation of $110,000 was used against a twenty-five-year life, which would allow four per cent straight-line depreciation. The declining balance method provided a six per cent rate of depreciation.

The twenty-five-year life will probably be questioned. It was used because the land is under-improved and it is reasonable to expect that the building would be removed and replaced with a more adequate improvement as the land value rises.

Note the way that line D declines. In the first year the depreciation is more than double the equity buildup, and in the ninth year the two are about equal.

Depreciation is "tax shelter," and when the time comes that it does not equal the equity buildup, then income tax will be paid on net income which is used to pay off the mortgage. The income tax paid will reduce "cash flow," which will force a reduction in cash distributions paid to investors.

Depreciation would be much larger if the proportion of building to land was larger, say 80 per cent building and 20 per cent land. Large depreciation can be taken in such a case, which usually applies to apartment buildings and taller structures.

The value of Exhibits 13-1 and 13-2 to the syndicate managers cannot be overestimated. Once these projections have been made and plotted, they can be altered to fit the current situation from time to time.

Projecting the capital gain potential

A projection of the capital gain potential, patterned after Exhibit 11-4 in Chapter 11, with periodic adjustments, furnishes a continual appraisal of the market value of the property, and the progress being made. Such a projection for the syndicate property must be kept up to date and should receive the closest attention from the syndicate managers.

Determining property management policy

Determination of property management policy is vital to the success of a real estate syndication.

There are differences of opinion about the management of real estate, and mention should be made of these so that the syndicate managers can formulate a management policy to be followed by the syndicate real estate manager.

These are some of the items about which there are differences of real estate management opinion:

Tenant selection: Some owners prefer top-rated tenants in clean lines of business, and others will accept tenants who are not so strong financially, and in lines of business which are considered to be high profit, but which are less desirable.

Financially strong, AAA type tenants will usually consider only 100 per cent locations, for which they want to pay low rents, get long leases and inducements such as free store fixtures.

Owners like the security of income of this type of tenant, but do not like the low rent and other demands.

The other extreme tenant choice consists of taking any tenant who can pay a high rent, almost without regard to the line of business or financial responsibility.

Syndicate management must decide the tenant selection policy by sensing the market for the space that they have to rent, matching this as closely as possible to syndicate goals, and then setting the tenant selection policy. Probably a compromise will be arrived at, largely determined by the availability of tenants and the demand for rentable space.

Rent collection: Some owners adopt a rigid collection policy, enforcing payment on or before the due dates as provided in the lease. Others take a slightly more lenient attitude. Policy must be set, to guide the real estate manager.

Repairs, maintenance and tenant service. The policy should be set, including the amount of any expenditure which can be made by the agent, without getting prior approval from the syndicators.

Rent statements and remittances of net rents. Set the policy so that there is no misunderstanding about when these are to be received by the syndicate managers.

Other items which come up with regard to building management policy should be considered, and the policy determined by the syndicate managers.

Analyzing the real estate

The syndicate managers should make frequent inspections of the property and of the area, and to make a sampling of the rental and sale market to keep their data updated.

Determining the depreciation schedule

Determination of the depreciation schedule is an owner-management decision which has to be decided only once, after seeking advice of competent tax counsel. The advisor should be familiar with the objectives of the syndicators and of the real estate syndicate. Usually the highest rate of depreciation which can be used is best for a real estate syndicate, providing the most "tax shelter."

Considering refinancing

Consideration of refinancing should be constantly kept in mind by the syndicate managers. The replacement of an existing loan with new financing at lower interest and for a longer period or better terms can increase net income.

Distributions to investors

Distributions to investors, and the timing of such payments are of importance to those who join in a real estate syndication. Monthly distributions can be a great attraction to some investors, while others are satisfied with quarterly payments of cash distributed. The policy must be set by the syndicate managers to match the proposals in the prospectus.

POINTS TO KEEP IN MIND

√ Management of the affairs of a real estate syndicate is concerned with setting syndicate policy, handling syndicate funds, keeping contact with participating investors to promote good public relations, directing the manager of syndicate owned real estate, working out tax saving programs, giving consideration to net income earned, and interpretation of the syndicate agreement to determine the distribution of cash profits to participating investors.

√ The management of syndicate owned real estate might be the responsibility of the syndicator who manages the affairs of the real estate syndicate, but it would only be that part of the responsibility which would ordinarily be delegated to a real estate management firm.

√ The syndicate management is charged with making forecasts of future prospects for syndicate owned real estate, projecting or approving of the rent schedules for income property, working out budgets for property improvements, and other tasks which would be performed by top level management.

√ The management of syndicate affairs is a responsibility which is similar to that of the board of directors of a corporation. The syndicate managers plan the deal, and the operation thereof, keep contact with the investors, manage the funds of the venture, and leave the execution of the day to day management of the syndicate owned real estate to hired, expert real estate managers who operate under the direction of the syndicate managers.

CHAPTER 14—

Management of Syndicate

Real Estate

The management of syndicated real estate can be divided into two classifications because of the types of property involved. The two types are:

1. Acreage or vacant land
2. Improved or income property

The following items concern a syndicator with relation to management of either type of real estate which would be owned by a real estate syndicate:

- The scope of the management job
- Determination of the type of manager needed
- Selection of the manager
- Resolving the management fee
- The management contract
- Employment of the real estate manager

ACREAGE OR VACANT LAND

The scope of the management job

The type of management needed by a real estate syndicate dealing in vacant land or acreage, and the scope of the management job depends on the objectives of the real estate syndicate.

There are acreage and vacant land syndicates which have as their objectives the conversion of high earned income into capital gain, and the deferment of payment of income tax until a subsequent year. The investors usually have high personal earnings, and desire to create expense such as prepaid interest for carrying vacant land, to sop up income in high earning periods. Then, at a later time or in a subsequent tax year, the land is sold to make a capital gain.

The management of real estate for this kind of a real estate syndicate is extremely simple, and, in fact consists only of collection of assessments from the investors with which to pay taxes and other carrying charges. Such land might be leased for agricultural use, or for some other purpose, in which event the manager would be expected to collect the rent for the syndicate.

The scope of the management of this type of real estate, for such syndicate aims, is simply to arrange to pay the carrying charges and wait for a favorable market in which to resell the property.

Other land syndicates have more complicated aims. One such type acquires land or acreage with the objective of working out all of the details of subdividing the property, except that the actual subdividing is left for a subsequent owner to do.

Such a syndicate might also be organized for the purpose of deferring payment of income tax on high earned personal income to convert it into capital gain, but uses the waiting period to get a tentative subdivision map approved if the land is on the fringe of a rapidly developing community.

After tentative subdivision maps receive approval of local planning authorities, portions of the land can be sold to residential subdivision construction companies for development, and to effect a partial capital gain for the syndicate.

The scope of the management job for this type of real estate syndicate would include handling the details of land subdivision, including arrangements for engineering and obtaining tentative approval of subdivision maps submitted to planning authorities.

Resale of syndicate real estate is part of the management job for either of the two types of land syndicate.

Determining the type of manager needed and selecting him

The manager for the simple land holding syndicate is usually the syndicator; no other manager is needed.

A much more sophisticated type of manager is needed for the land syndicate which has as its objective the division of land into parcels for subdivision purposes. Arrangements for engineering the land are complicated, and steering the plot plans through the governmental agencies to get tentative approval and necessary zoning requires that the manager have special skills.

A syndicate holding real estate with subdivision as the objective should employ a land development firm.

Resolving the management fee

The manager of real estate for a simple land-holding syndicate has a job with few responsibilities. Usually the syndicator, or one of them, manages the syndicate real estate.

Even this simple management takes time, and there are always "out-of-pocket" expenses connected with the job.

One land syndicator told me that he managed a couple of syndicates without being compensated for the work, but he found that it was time-consuming and there were expenses involved. Thereafter he made a charge of 1.5 per cent of the cost of the land for each year that the land was held, to cover his expenses, which included inspection of the land, pictures, reports, subscription to local newspapers and collections for payment of syndicate bills.

Land development syndicates have different management problems.

There are syndicators who can raise the money to acquire land for the purpose of setting up contemplated subdivisions in the path of progress of a fast-developing community, but who cannot themselves manage the development phase of the syndication.

This is a situation which requires the employment of competent land developing talent.

Land development is a specialized business. A real estate syndicate dealing in land needs the judgment, knowledge and ability of a land developer for best results.

The land development real estate syndicate which has a land development specialist as one of the syndicators is fortunate indeed.

An individual land developer or a development firm can manage a number of deals simultaneously. The volume of business makes multiple use of research time.

The fee to be paid to a land development specialist is negotiable. There are those who will only work for a set fee, some who work on a time basis, and the ones who want a share of the profits to be made.

The syndicators choose the deal which appears to be best for their venture.

The management contract and employment of a land manager

The management contract for a simple land syndication where the syndicators, or one of them, manage the syndicate real estate is usually incorporated as part of the syndicate agreement. The deal is just to acquire acreage or vacant land, pay the carrying expenses, and sell for capital appreciation. The syndicate agreement covers the fee for management of the real estate.

Employment of a professional land developer, or firm, by a real estate syndicate whose activities require his help entails entering into a management contract which covers the arrangements between the parties. The contract should be prepared by legal counsel employed by the syndicators.

IMPROVED, OR INCOME PROPERTY

Improved, or income property of any size requires skilled management to get the most out of it.

There are a large number of different types of income property, and there are real estate management firms which specialize in each of the types.

In the instance of the 4000 Redbird Boulevard property, it happened that one of the syndicators was a manager of commercial property, and so the management of the property was delegated to him.

Suppose, however, that these two syndicators had found a bargain in an industrial property which they felt was suitable for syndication. The property might be leased to strong, reliable tenants for long terms on lease, and in this event the management would only consist of receiving rent and paying a few bills. This job could then also be delegated to Jones, one of the syndicators.

The industrial property might have leasing problems, or remodeling, possibly additional construction, would be needed. This situation would make the syndicators give thought to the employment of an industrial property management specialist, whose familiarity with the problems would be invaluable.

Syndicators should be mindful that a real estate syndicate dealing in income property is a business which demands the best management available, even if help must be obtained from an outside source.

The scope of the management job

The scope of the management job for each type of income property is different. As an example of the services to be rendered by a management firm, I have included as Exhibit 14-1 a copy of the form of management contract which was used to delegate the management of a sizable commercial and office building in Chicago to a large real estate management firm. Absentee owners turned over the entire management of the property to this agent by the use of this management contract, which describes the agent's duties.

Determination of the type of manager needed

The syndicators make this judgment. The management of any type of real estate where the whole job consists of depositing rent checks and paying a few bills is so simple that no professional help is needed. A complicated or specialized management job needs the services of a specialist in the particular field.

Selection of the manager

Selection of the manager for income property by the syndicators involves weighing the merits of the managers who are available, the convenience of their office location, the ability of the agent to handle leasing if vacancies occur, and the financial responsibility of the agent being considered. Selection of a real estate manager for syndicated property is an important executive decision to be made by the syndicators after due consideration of all the factors involved.

Resolving the management fee

The management fee and leasing commissions are the subject of negotiation by the syndicators with the managing agent selected. Fees vary in different areas, but they are fairly standardized locally and can usually be pretty well established by contacting a local real estate board.

The management contract

Exhibit 14-1 is a copy of the real estate management contract or agreement previously mentioned. It is a sample showing what could reasonably be expected to be covered in such an agreement.

EXHIBIT 14-1

MANAGEMENT AGREEMENT

In consideration of the covenants herein contained _____, (hereinafter called " Owner ") and _____, (hereinafter called " Agent ") agree as follows :

1. The Owner hereby employs the Agent exclusively to manage, operate and rent the property located and known as _____ .

In the City of _____ State of _____ upon the terms hereinafter set forth, for the period of one year beginning on the _____ day of _____ 19___, and thereafter for yearly periods. Said contract may be canceled by either Agent or Owner upon thirty (30) days' written notice of intention to do so, with no penalty to owner for unexpired term of leases.

2. The Agent agrees :
   a. To accept and hereby does accept the said employment for the periods and upon the terms herein provided, and agrees to furnish the services of its organization for the renting, operating and managing of said premises.
   b. To employ and supervise all labor required for the operation and maintenance of the premises.
   c. To investigate carefully all references of prospective tenants.
   d. To render to the Owner monthly statements of receipts, disbursements ond charges. The balance of funds remaining after such disbursements are to be remitted to the Owner within ten days after the end of each month. In case the disbursements shall be in excess of the rents collected by the Agent, the Owner agrees to pay such excess promptly upon demand.

3. The Owner hereby gives to the Agent the following authority and powers, and agrees to assume the expense incurred in connection therewith :
   a. To collect all rents due or to become due and receipt therefore : to sue for and attempt to recover delinquent rents; to institute and prosecute actions to oust tenants and to recover possession of the premises ; and when expedient, to settle, compromise and release such actions or rights of actions ; to advertise in newspapers and by signs on the premises ; and rent said premises or any part thereof.
   b. To hire, direct, discharge and pay all employees ; to make or cause to be made repairs and alterations and to order and supervise all decorating of the premises ; to purchase supplies and to pay all bills.

4. The Owner further agrees :
   a. To save the Agent harmless from all damage suits in connection with the management of the property and from liability for injuries suffered by any employee or other person whomsoever, and to carry at his own expense, public liability, elevator liability, and steam

boiler insurance adequate to protect the interests of the parties hereto, which policies shall be so written as to protect the Agents in the same manner and to the same extent as the Owner.

b. To pay the Agent each month:
FOR SERVICE: _____ (_____%) per cent of the gross amount of money received from the operation of said premises during the period herein provided for.

c. To keep such records as may be necessary in order to comply with the Social Security Act or any other Federal or State Legislation.

No agreement or understandings regarding the subject matter of this contract other than those expressed herein or otherwise in writing and signed by each party shall be deemed to exist or to bind either of the parties hereto.

This agreement shall be binding upon the successors and assigns of the Agent, and the heirs, administrators, executors, successors, and assigns of the Owner.

In WITNESS WHEREOF, the parties hereto have affixed or caused to be affixed their respective signatures this _____ day of _____ 19____ .

BY: _____ SEAL
                        Owner

BY: _____ SEAL
                        Agent

Employment of the real estate manager

The employment of a real estate manager who will be in charge of real estate owned by a real estate syndicate is accomplished by deciding the scope of the management job, determining the type of manager needed, selecting the manager who appears to be best qualified, negotiating the management fee, preparing the management contract, and then hiring the real estate manager. See Chapter 6 for general guidelines to hiring a manager of syndicate owned real estate.

POINTS TO KEEP IN MIND

√ There is a vast difference between management of real estate by an agent who only expects to collect the rents and pay the bills of managed property, as against management of property by a qualified, expert real estate manager, who gives each managed property his close attention in order to get the most out of the operation for his principal.

√ Owners of real estate are notably cost conscious, and usually do not realize that they could be losing money and potential capital gain by employing the lowest priced management of their property.

√ The successful management of real estate by a managing agent is a job which involves the collection of rent and payment of bills, but, in addition to these duties, a competent manager would keep in touch with rental values, repair costs, vacancy factors, neighborhood changes and developments. The high type managing agent uses his knowledge for the benefit of the owner of the property, and uses imagination in seeking tenants who can make the best use of available rentable space at the highest possible rents. He plans for the future, to increase net revenue, and thus to increase the value of the property.

√ Competent management costs more, but is worth more.

√ A Syndicator should give serious consideration to the qualifications of a real estate manager who is to be employed to operate syndicate owned real estate. Employment of the right managing agent can be the key to successful real estate syndication.

CHAPTER 15—

Reports to Investors

THE IMPORTANCE OF REPORTS TO INVESTORS

Every business organization recognizes that investors expect to get periodic reports concerning the business in which they have a financial interest.

Large corporations furnish their stockholders with elaborate quarterly and annual reports which show the financial condition, earnings, progress and future prospects of the company, as compared with previous years' operations, and with the competition. These reports are expensive, but necessary. They keep the stockholders informed, interested, and presumably satisfied. Informed, satisfied investors are good advertisers for the organization in which they have invested their money.

Syndicators face the same business problem of keeping investors in a real estate syndicate informed, interested and satisfied with the conduct of their business venture.

Real estate syndicates usually operate with two types of property, acreage or vacant land and income property. Each type of property requires a different, but similar, kind of reporting to investors.

For purposes of illustration, I have set up a simulated syndication of acreage, the format consisting of a limited partnership called the Old Ranch Partnership, for which examples of reports to investors will be exhibited. The 4000 Redbird Boulevard property will be the subject for the income property syndication, with the 4000 Redbird Associates limited partnership as the organizational vehicle. Examples of reports which could be used with reference to this type of real estate syndication will be included.

These are the reports which a syndicator should make to investors:

For a Vacant Land or Acreage Syndicate:

- Syndicator's first report to investors
- The quarterly report
- The annual report

130

For the Income Property Syndicate:
- Syndicator's first report to investors
- The monthly report
- The annual report

This is the way that a syndicator's reports could be prepared for a vacant land or acreage syndicate

VACANT LAND SYNDICATE—REPORTS TO INVESTORS

Syndicator's first report to investors

This report, in the form of a review of the transaction for the acquisition of the property, the aims of the syndicate and a budget showing the projection of expenditures from the amount raised by the syndication, gives every participant in the syndicate a clear picture of the beginning of the venture. See Exhibit 15-1.

EXHIBIT 15-1

REPORT TO PARTICIPANTS OF
OLD RANCH PARTNERSHIP

January 1, 19_____.

The Old Ranch Partnership, in which you are a participant as a Limited Partner, has, as of this date, entered into a contract to purchase land on the fringe of development at the north end of the City of Fandango, California.

The land, known for years as the "Old Ranch," consists of 200 acres, now used for cattle grazing, situated between Seaside Road and the Pacific Ocean. The slightly rolling contour is ideal for residential subdivision.

Utilities are available to the property, and water-sewer service can be had by extension of existing mains.

The Partnership has been formed to control the land by means of a purchase agreement. The agreement which was executed by the General Partners provides for a 10% down payment and up to nine succeeding annual payments of 10% or more of the purchase price. Interest on unpaid balance of principal, at the rate of 7% per annum, is to be prepaid for the first two years, with up to eight annual payments of interest on the unpaid balance of principal, beginning at the end of the first year. Provision has been made for the Seller to release any parcel which the Partnership requires for resale, by payment of pro-rata unpaid purchase price per acre to be so released.

Tentative zoning for residential use is to be sought, so that resale of portions of the tract can be made to residential construction companies.

When property resales have been completed, the cash contributions of capital made by partners will be repaid out of the proceeds of resales. Profit, if any, thereafter, is to be divided, 80% to Limited Partners and 20% to General Partners, as provided in the Partnership Agreement.

The total consideration to be paid for the Old Ranch is the sum of $500,000.00, being 200 acres at $2,500 per acre. The down payment was $50,000.

The sum of $150,000.00 was raised by contributions of capital by the partners of Old Ranch Partnership. This has been budgeted for the first year as follows:

BUDGET

Old Ranch Partnership

Operations 1/1/19_____ to 12/31/19_____.

Down Payment on purchase—Old Ranch	$ 50,000.00
1st year's prepaid interest—7% × $450,000 =	31,500.00
2nd year's ″ —7% × 400,000 =	28,000.00
Real estate tax—1st year	3,000.00
Organizational expense, reimbursement	3,000.00
Management—1½% × $500,000	7,500.00
Working surplus—to be used for land engineering, water & sewer main extensions, etc.	$ 27,000.00
	$150,000.00

The quarterly report

A quarterly report, like the one shown in Exhibit 15-2, shows the financial transactions for the period, also includes an account of the progress made toward the achievement of the aims of the syndicate. This quarterly report is for the purpose of maintaining good public relations with the participants in the syndicate. It shows that the capital contributed by the partners is being wisely expended for the benefit of the group.

EXHIBIT 15-2

OLD RANCH PARTNERSHIP
First Quarterly Report

March 31, 19_____.

The Old Ranch Partnership contracted to purchase the Old Ranch as of January 1, 19_____, at a purchase price of $500,000, of which $50,000 was paid to the Seller as a down payment.

The budget as set up by the General Partners provided for the operations of the Partnership during the first year as follows:

BUDGET

Down payment	$ 50,000.00
1st year's prepaid interest	31,500.00
2nd "	28,000.00
Organizational expense	3,000.00
Real estate tax, 1st year	3,000.00
Management fee	7,500.00
Working surplus, for land engineering, etc.	27,000.00
Total amount contributed to capital by partners	$150,000.00
Paid out at closing of contract, first four items	112,500.00
Cash in National Bank after close of contract, 1/1/19_____.	$37,500.00

Immediately after taking possession of the Old Ranch, the General Partners let a contract to Engineering Associates for engineering the land into lots of one acre gross size, which gross size would include streets and easements. Division of the ranch into parcels or tracts was a part of the engineering contract. The engineering has now been completed and paid for in full as shown on the Operating Statement.

OLD RANCH PARTNERSHIP

Operating Statement

Period January 1, 19_____ to March 31, 19_____.

Cash in National Bank as of 1/1/19_____.		$37,500.00
Disbursements :		
Engineering Associates	$10,000.00	
Blank County—Filing for rezoning	200.00	
Insurance Agency—Liability Ins.	300.00	
Land Development Co. (General Partner)		
Management—1/1 to 3/31/19_____.	1,875.00	
Total expenditures 1st quarter 19 _____.		$12,375.00
Cash in National Bank as of 3/31/19_____.		$25,125.00

REPORT OF PROGRESS

The Partnership is ahead of schedule with the procedures which should lead to establishing tentative subdivision maps and the rezoning of the Old Ranch property.

Negotiations are under way with the owner of a large tract adjacent to Old Ranch on the south, for the sharing of the original cost of extending water and sewer mains to serve both properties. Estimates for extension of these facilities are being prepared by the water and sewer district engineers, and should be available within a short time.

The adjacent owner has indicated that he would pay one half of the cost of extending these mains. The Partnership had anticipated advancing approximately $18,000 for main extensions, which would be partially reimbursed as others connected to the mains. The deal with the neighbor would save about $9,000 at this time.

Sales of acreage in the vicinity of Old Ranch have been made since the Partnership took possession. Smaller tracts, 50 acres or less, have been sold at over $3,000 per acre.

The University has let a contract for a $6 million building. Several large research and development companies are negotiating for locations on industrially zoned land which is about two miles away from Old Ranch.

There has been some inquiry by real estate brokers with regard to a resale of the ranch, but the General Partners are firmly convinced that adherence to the original aims of the Partnership, i. e., resale of parcels ofter rezoning, will produce a handsome capital gain for the Partnership.

THE OLD RANCH PARTNERSHIP

By—Land Development Co.

General Partner

EXHIBIT 15-2 (CONTINUED)

The annual report

The syndicator operating an acreage or vacant land syndicate should employ an accountant to make an annual audit, and also prepare a financial report for the participants together with partnership income tax returns.

The financial report and income tax returns should be forwarded to the partners promptly so that they can incorporate the taxable income into their personal income tax returns.

A report of the progress made during the year should be made in form similar to the quarterly report, Exhibit 15-2. The annual report to investors should include a statement of items to be paid in the second year of operation. This statement could be similar to the budget portion of Exhibit 15-2.

This budget is the basis for assessments due from the participating limited partners, and in the case of the Old Ranch Partnership the syndicator or general partner would have sent each limited partner a bill for his share of the $84,000 total. Each participant would be expected to remit $8,400 prior to the end of the first year so that the obligations of the partnership could be promptly met. The statement of assessment due should be itemized.

A fully informed group is always easily handled. These participants will have been fully briefed as to the format of the Old Ranch Partnership, they will have executed the partnership agreement, which recites the particulars of the deal, and they will have received an initial report, quarterly reports, an audit and an annual report.

EXHIBIT 15-3

BUDGET

OLD RANCH PARTNERSHIP

Operations 1/1/19_____ to 12/31/19_____.

Interest on $350,000 @ 7% for 3rd year	$24,500.00
Real estate taxes, year 19_____.	3,000.00
Management fee, 2nd year	7,500.00
Total expense, 2nd year	$34,000.00
Principal payment, 2nd year	50,000.00
Total amount to be assessed to Limited Partners	$84,000.00
Due from each Limited Partner in the Old Ranch Partnership 10% × $84,000 =	$8,400.00

INCOME PROPERTY SYNDICATE—
REPORTS TO INVESTORS

The building to be used in this example is the 4000 Redbird property, 4000 Redbird Associates owner, a limited partnership patterned after the sample agreement shown in Exhibit 8-2, the Prospectus, Chapter 8.

Exhibit 10-4, Chapter 10 describes the property. The purchase price of $175,000 requires that $72,200 be raised by syndication. Profits from operations are to be split 80 per cent to limited partners and 20 per cent to general partners.

Syndicator's first report to investors

This report can be a simple letter from the general partners, making note of the deal closing, including a copy of the escrow statement and the summary which shows the disposition of funds raised by the syndication and the cash in the bank on the day that the partnership took over the operation of the property.

EXHIBIT 15-4

BLANK TITLE COMPANY

Escrow Statement of 4000 Redbird Associates 12/1/64

Property located—4000 Redbird Blvd.	Debits	Credits
Deposit		$ 65,781.67
Consideration	$175,000.00	
Principal balance first trust deed		107,947.20
Adjustments :		
Taxes—$ 3,351.28 per 12 mo. from 12/1/64 to 12/31/64	279.41	
Insurance—$571.31 per year— from 12/1/64 to 5/31/65	285.66	
Rents	—0—	—0—
Interest	—0—	—0—
Lease security deposits		2,040.00
Recording documents	2.80	
Escrow fee	201.00	
	$175,768.87	$175,768.87

SUMMARY

Amount raised by syndication		$ 72,200.00
Demand to close deal	$ 65,781.67	
Organization expense—to S. Smith	3,000.00	68,781.67
Total cash in bank 12/1/64		$ 3,418.33
Lease security deposits—to be segregated		2,040.00
Working surplus		$ 1,378.33

The monthly report

This report should consist of a copy of the managing agent's rent statement, a statement of operations of the property from the beginning of the fiscal year to date and a financial summary showing cash on hand at beginning of fiscal year and at the end of the month being reported. Exhibits 15-5, 15-6, and 15-7, respectively, are samples of these statements, and are also used as parts of the annual report to investors.

Distributions of cash to investors should be shown in the report as a total. For instance, in the case of the 4000 Redbird building a monthly distribution to each limited partner of $70 per month would be logical and feasible. Should this arrangement have been made, then a check for $70 would be included with each monthly report to limited partners, and the total of such distributions would be shown on the financial summary

EXHIBIT 15-5

4000–4016 Redbird Blvd. Bldg.
Owner: 4000 Redbird Blvd. Associates

JOHN J. JONES
Real Estate Management
22 "A" STREET
VENTURA, CALIFORNIA

RENT STATEMENT
FOR PERIOD FROM 11/1/65   TO 11/30/65

DUE BEGINNING OF MONTH	TENANT		RENT CURRENT MO.	OTHER CHARGES	COLLECTIONS	DATE	ADJUSTMENTS & ALLOWANCES	DUE END OF MONTH
	Clipper Club 4000 Redbird Blvd.	11/30/68	425.00		425.00	11/2		
	Barber 4002 Redbird Blvd.	11/30/68	125.00		125.00	11/1		
	Beauty Shop 4004 Redbird Blvd.	11/30/68	250.00		250.00	11/5/		
	Auto Finance 4006 Redbird Blvd.	11/30/68	240.00		240.00	11/4		
	Furniture 4008 Redbird Blvd. 4010 " " 4012 " "	11/30/68	700.00		700.00	11/10		
	Savings & Loan 4016 Redbird Blvd.	4/30/66	300.00		300.00	11/1		
					$ 2,040.00			

4000–4016 Redbird Blvd. Bldg.
Owner: 4000 Redbird Blvd. Associates

JOHN J. JONES
Real Estate Management
22 "A" STREET
VENTURA, CALIFORNIA

DISBURSEMENTS
FOR PERIOD FROM 11/1/65   TO 11/30/65

DATE	CHECK NO.	PAID TO	DESCRIPTION	CHARGES
11/5	1065	Parking Sweeping Service	Parking maintenance	$ 20.00
11/15	1126	So. Calif. Edison	Electricity	34.19
11/30	1205	John J. Jones	Management fee November	99.50
11/30	1206	4000 Redbird Blvd. Assoc.	Balance– November rents	$ 1,886.31

to the date of the report. Payments to general partners, and adjustments to divide the "cash flow" 80 per cent to limited partners and 20 per cent to general partners are made at the end of the fiscal year.

A letter from the general partners should accompany the monthly report, telling of any progress made or interesting news about the property or neighborhood.

The annual report

Include the managing agent's last monthly rent statement, Exhibit 15-5; a statement of operations for the fiscal year, Exhibit 15-6; a financial summary, Exhibit 15-7; a computation of net income credited to partner's accounts, Exhibit 15-8 and a covering letter from the general partners informing the limited partners of developments during the year which affect the subject property.

The annual report should be prepared by an accountant, as the result of an audit of the operations of the partnership, and it should be accompanied by a copy of the partnership income tax return, so that the participating partners can incorporate the figures into their personal income tax returns.

EXHIBIT 15-6

4000 REDBIRD ASSOCIATES

Statement of Operations

4000—4016 Redbird Blvd. Building

Fiscal Year—12/1/64 to 11/30/65

Total rents collected by Agent		$23,930.00
Expenses:		
Paid by Agent:		
Parking maintenance	$240.00	
Utilities	206.66	
Repairs	129.76	
Unclassified	8.35	
Management	1,196.50	
Total paid by Agent		$1,781.27
Paid from Partnership Account:		
Interest	$5,860.60	
Real estate tax	3,350.00	
Insurance, fire/liability	571.31	
Total paid by Partnership		$9,781.91
TOTAL EXPENSES		$11,563.18
NET INCOME		$12,366.82
Principal payment, lst trust deed		3,224.80
"CASH FLOW"—available for distributions to investors		$ 9,142.02

EXHIBIT 15-7

4000 REDBIRD ASSOCIATES

Financial Summary

Fiscal year 12/1/64 to 11/30/65

12/1/64	Cash in Bank		
Lease security deposits			$ 2,040.00
Working Surplus			1,378.33
Total cash in bank 12/1/64			$ 3,418.33
"Cash Flow" (from Annual Statement)			9,142.02
			$12,560.35
Distribution of cash to Limited Partners—80% × $9,142.02		$ 7,313.62	
Distribution of cash to General Partners—20% × $9,142.02		1,828.40	$ 9,142.02
Total cash in bank 11/30/65			$ 3,418.33
Lease security deposits			2,040.00
Working surplus			$ 1,378.33

EXHIBIT 15-8

Net Income Credited to Partners' Accounts

	Total	80% to Limited Partners' Accounts	20% to General Partners' Accounts
Net Income	$12,366.82	$9,893.46	$2,473.36
Depreciation	6,600.00	5,280.00	1,320.00
Taxable	$ 5,766.82	$4,613.46	$1,153.36

Distribution of "Cash Flow."

	Total	80%	20%
Net Income	$12,366.82	$9,893.46	$2,473.36
Mortgage Payoff	3,224.80	2,579.84	644.96
"Cash Flow"	$ 9,142.02	$7,313.62	$1,828.40

Net Income on $9,000 Limited Partnership Interest
Net Income—1/8 × $9,893.46 $1,211.68 = 13.46% earned
Depreciation—1/8 × $5,280.00   660.00

Taxable $ 551.68

Cash Distribution on $9,000 Limited Partnership Interest

1/8 × $ 7,313.62 $ 914.20 = 10.15% paid
Taxable   551.68

" Tax Shelter " $ 362.52

EXHIBIT 15-8 (CONTINUED)

The comprehensive annual report to investors is for the purpose of keeping the participants in the partnership informed of the affairs of the venture to such a degree that there are no questions to be asked of the general partners, who manage the business of the partnership.

The partnership income tax return contains practically the same information, but it is my experience that investors simply turn this return over to their tax counsel without inspecting it.

The importance of reports to investors cannot be overemphasized.

POINTS TO KEEP IN MIND

√ Reports to participating investors should commence immediately after a real estate syndicate becomes operational.

√ The reports from the syndicator managers to the participating investors demonstrate to them that the affairs of the syndicate are receiving proper attention.

√ Periodic reports to investors give them a sense of ownership in the project. Reports showing an operating profit give them a sense of pride in their ownership participation in a real estate syndicate.

√ Reports from the syndicator managers are essential to the participating investors in order that the investors can take advantage of tax benefits in their income tax returns.

CHAPTER 16—

How to Increase Value

of Property

All owners of real estate would like to know how to increase the value of their property. The reason that most owners never learn how to increase the value of property is that there is no established technique which can be acquired, from which positive results can be expected.

The owners of small properties do not have the imagination, the knowledge or skills which would enable them to increase the value of their property, and they often do not have the money to do the job when they do know how to do it.

The owners of large properties do have the financial capacity to manage property so that the value will increase, but owners of such real estate tend to employ real estate managers on the basis of the lowest charge for the service. Few owners are willing to pay the price for outstanding management ability.

The amount which a syndicator can make out of a real estate syndication depends on his ability to do an outstanding job of management of the syndicate. He is obligated to try by every available means to increase the value of syndicate property. This may mean the employment of a real estate manager other than himself, but the stakes are too high to accept second-rate management service, or, in fact to accept any second-rate service which might weaken the efforts of the syndicator to increase property value of syndicate real estate.

The syndicator is a specialist who makes a study of the syndicate property, and makes use of every influence which he can bring to bear to increase the value of the property, because he makes money only if the participating investors make profits.

HOW TO INCREASE VALUE OF PROPERTY

Acreage or vacant land:

- Wait for prices to increase
- Subdivide
- Rezone
- Improve the land
- Develop the land
- Advocate public improvements
- Explore for natural resources
- Lease the property

Income Property:

- Add improvements
- Remodel
- Advertise
- Increase rents
- Supply automobile parking
- Refinance

ACREAGE OR VACANT LAND

Wait for prices to increase

This is a technique used by syndicators to obtain an increase in the value of land which has been acquired in a rising price market.

The technique consists of group purchase of land, using the capital of participating investors who are in high personal income tax brackets to control the property. The expense of carrying the land is charged against the high earned incomes of the participants, to reduce their personal income taxes. The share of expense which each participant pays to carry the land is therefore reduced by the income tax he would have paid on that amount.

A rapid increase in the value of acreage or vacant land is probable if residential and industrial activity builds up in the area. Demand, scarcity and inflation are some of the influences which would accelerate this trend.

A syndicator who controls acreage or vacant land by syndication can increase the value of the property by simply waiting for from three to five years, during which time the real estate is being carried at low expense.

Subdivide

Subdivision is one way to increase the value of vacant land or acreage. The smaller the units can be made, the more the price per acre of land increases. Syndication of subdivisions is common practice.

Rezoning and installation of necessary land improvements are a part of this method of increasing the value of land by subdivision.

Some syndicators bring the work of subdividing up to the point of actually doing it, and then sell off fairly large parcels to residential construction companies which finish the job of subdividing and build the houses.

This method of increasing the value of the syndicate property utilizes the period which would ordinarily be required for the value of the land to increase for the purpose of obtaining tentative approval of rezoning and subdivision of the property.

The syndicate gets a higher price for the land, which is ready for almost immediate utilization by a construction company which builds houses.

Rezone

Rezoning land to a more intensive use is a potent way to increase the value of property. Rezoning agricultural land for residential use can easily double or triple the value of the property.

Rezoning single-family residential land to apartment use, or obtaining more liberal commercial or industrial zoning for land, can increase value. Rezoning for tall building use can produce dramatic price changes.

I have attended a great many sessions of local planning commissions, and never fail to find one or more of the applicants for rezoning to be syndicators. They seek more liberal zoning on property which they control, and then resell for capital gain, develop the property or subdivide.

Rezoning can be very rewarding to a real estate syndicate, and to a syndicator. Rezoning almost never fails to increase the value of property.

Improve the land

Improvement of land by installation of sewers, supplying water, providing public utilities and building roads adds far more to the value of land which is in demand than the cost of installing these services. Subdivision of land into small lots is practically impossible without sewers, for instance.

Changing the contour of the land can be very rewarding both in appearance and usability of the land. Ravines and gullies can be filled when underground drainage is provided. Converting "rough" land into usable residential land can greatly increase the value.

Landscaping can be important. The planting or removal of trees and shrubbery can make a great difference in the attractiveness of property, and can increase the value.

Protective fences and walls are becoming increasingly valuable as attractions to residents and industrial users of land. A tract of land which has a protective wall around it can be much more valuable to the users.

Each parcel of vacant land or acreage has its own characteristics, and in every community the users of land have different requirements. Study the situation to make land improvements which will most effectively increase the value and desirability of the land to get increased profits.

Develop the land

Development of land by building houses or other buildings on it makes the land more valuable.

For some years I was involved with the improvement of commercial land, constructing comparatively small store buildings, leasing them, and then selling them after a year or two of operation. Most of the increase in the value of these properties was in the land. Neighboring parcels of vacant commercially zoned land went up in value almost as much as the property which had been developed. In fact the vacant land which was left could command higher rents from tenants who wanted to get into the already developed area. Of course the stores which were first built did produce rent during the holding period, while the vacant parcels were a continuing expense to the owners while carrying.

The development of land by building on it can be very profitable, but the job is complicated with necessary planning, financing, supervision of construction, leasing or selling. There are loan fees to pay, interest under construction, possible loss of rent before the property is fully occupied, and there is always the chance that the income when the building is completed and fully rented will not come up to expectations.

I always felt that a developer of income property was entitled to a return of about 25 per cent on invested capital, especially if the developer handled most of the detail work himself. The first year of operation usually does not produce this rate of return because of the time and rent lost while getting tenants for the building.

A syndicator who undertakes the development of vacant land on behalf of a real estate syndicate should understand that he is starting a going business, which entails risks.

The syndicator who develops income property for a syndicate should carefully plan the venture, obtain a feasibility report from a reliable source, and plan the project with an architect who knows how to design the improvements so that their operation can be profitable. He must get firm commitments for adequate financing, time the project so that it is completed at an advantageous time and use aggressive renting methods. The participating investors should be able and willing to make further contributions of capital if required to carry the venture until it becomes operational.

Development of income property is a logical purpose of real estate syndication, and can be very profitable. Overoptimism should be avoided. Plenty of safety factors should be provided with regard to timing of the various operations to be done, the cost of financing and the time for renting a development project "to be built."

Development of property increases the value of this property and almost always does the same for nearby undeveloped land.

Advocate public improvements

Every active area in which a syndicator would have interest has a public improvement program worked out. Inquiry at the offices of the governmental agencies which handle these programs enables an alert syndicator to study the effect of the programs on his syndicate property.

Pressure from the syndicator can often divert a project which might have an adverse influence on the syndicate property, or could influence the authorities to locate the improvement so that it adds to the value of the subject real estate.

Public improvements, such as roads, bridges, schools, recreation facilities, water storage with sport potential—all of these can exert a powerful influence on the value of nearby real estate.

An astute use of persuasion by the syndicator to get public improvements located to his advantage can produce a large increase in value of syndicate property.

Explore for natural resources

Every syndicator who deals in the syndication of acreage or vacant land should make a careful check of the possibility of the discovery of valuable natural resources on the land.

Most people think in terms of the discovery of oil, gas or minerals, but there are other resources which can be very valuable.

Sand, stone, rock, diatomaceous earth, slate, water and many other natural resources can have great value, and the discovery could increase property value.

A depression in the land can be used to dispose of material removed from excavations, and if the material which is accepted can be compacted, the hole, ravine or depression can be converted to valuable use.

Trees can be cut and sold for timber. One parcel of land in which I had an interest was improved with a large residence and lush landscaping. The house cost $5,000 to get rid of, but the landscaping was worth $25,000 to $30,000, and specimen plants could have been sold at big prices.

Natural resources can enhance the value of property. Look for them.

Lease the property

Vacant land or acreage can be increased in value if it can be leased, or rented.

Acreage can be leased for agricultural use, for grazing of cattle, exploration for oil and minerals and for many other uses.

Vacant land in and near cities can be leased for the sale of used automobiles, landscaping materials, building materials, for gasoline stations and many other purposes.

Any land which can command an income is more valuable than it was before a use could be found for it.

INCOME PROPERTY

Add improvements

The addition of improvements to income property can add value which is all out of proportion to the cost involved.

Landscaping could make a commercial or apartment property so much more attractive that the rents could be raised.

There are those who feel that a swimming pool has a real attraction for tenants, and an atmosphere value which dwarfs the cost of the pool.

Additional rentable space can often be built which brings in additional revenue and increases the value of the property.

Adding to the improvements on an income property costs money, which usually cannot be paid for out of the rents. A syndicator should provide for the cost of improvements when the syndicate is formed so that assessments will not have to be paid by the participants in the venture, when needed improvements are made.

Improvements can produce startling results in increased rents and added value to income property. Every consideration should be given to this subject by a syndicator.

Remodel

There are properties which can be bought which have a great potential and the value of the holding can be greatly increased by a judicious expenditure of capital for remodeling.

This is especially true of commercial property. The addition of new store fronts can change the whole character of a building, even if it is several stories high, because people seldom look above the first floor of a building.

There have been times in my management experience when a tenant was required to allow the remodeling of his store front, and to pay additional rent for a renewal of his lease when this improvement had been made. Without exception, the tenants who were required to spruce up their stores did more business. Some even paid excess percentage rent as a result of the improved appearance of the store.

Remodeling of residential property should be approached with caution. The job, once started, seems to have no ending. There is so much equipment in the modern apartment which can become obsolete that the expense of replacing it and modernizing the interior and exterior of such a building can be excessive. Remodeling of residential space requires that it be vacated while the work is in progress, causing a loss of rent.

A thorough cleanup and painting of the exterior of an apartment building and of the public areas usually produces the greatest increase of rent for money expended. Increased rent increases the value of property.

Advertise

Advertising increases the value of income property because the public then becomes aware of it, and of the worth of the space being offered for rent. The demand for space which is for rent makes it possible to increase rents. When the property is being offered for resale, the increased rents can be advertised to attract buyers for the property.

The value of advertising in increasing value of property can be demonstrated by my observation of certain residential properties in the city of Santa Barbara, California.

These properties are of the group ownership or cooperative type, owned by prosperous individuals.

When the properties were developed, an active advertising campaign sold them all out within a reasonable time, and at prices comparable to individual residences in the area.

Now there are some resales available in almost all of the cooperative developments in the city, but these resales are being handled by the individual owners, who are reluctant to spend the money to present them properly to prospective buyers by means of suitable advertising. The sellers are gradually becoming discouraged, and lowering their prices. Very few sales have resulted because the public has not been informed that these bargains are available.

Advertising can cause an increase in the value of property which is for sale, because the publicity creates a demand for the space or for the property.

Increase rents

I have advocated frequent checking of rents and real estate prices in areas surrounding property which is of interest to a syndicator. I point out that in the case of the 4000 Redbird Boulevard building, it was assumed that the rents were too low, but that most of the leases would expire within four years after the purchase of the property.

The graph (see Exhibit 11-4, Chapter 11) projects the increase in the value of the property if rents were to be increased to the prevailing area rents when leases expire.

A syndicator always aims to get the highest rent obtainable from acceptable tenants without causing undue loss of rent or vacancy.

Gross rent can sometimes be increased by furnishing additional services, but this usually leads to giving free services to all tenants.

A rent increase which does not increase expense reduces the proportion between expense and gross income. A property with a low percentage of expense impresses prospective buyers. Such a property can be sold in the higher range of the price spread.

Always increase rents if and when possible in order to increase the value of the subject property.

There are rent increases which come about because of provisions in current leases or in new leases when negotiated. Graduated increases in rents where leases run for periods of several years are common. There is no set pattern for graduating rent increases. Sometimes the graduation is made to accommodate a tenant with a slightly lower rent for the first year or so of a lease, then increasing the rent in one or more steps to average out so that the effects of inflation and the increased value of the location are reflected in the total rent paid for the term.

Percentage rents sometimes produce rent increases. The use of a percentage of gross sales to determine the rent to be paid by a tenant, working against a minimum rent to be paid, can produce more rent and thus increase the value of a building to some degree. Most prospective buyers give no consideration to excess rents as an indication of added value of the building.

Tenants who are rated AAA very seldom make leases which produce excess rentals over the minimum rent which has to be paid.

My experience over a period of many years indicates that percentage leases appear to protect owners of property against inflation and of underestimating the true potential of a location, but that they seldom produce much cash income.

Rent increases do increase the value of property and do increase the net income, which is the gauge of value of income property.

Supply automobile parking

Furnishing automobile parking is an inducement offered by owners of commercial and apartment properties to obtain tenants.

The use of land for the purpose of furnishing free automobile parking obligates an owner for the duration of leases which provide for such service.

Free automobile parking does attract tenants to apartment and commercial buildings in locations which would otherwise be difficult to rent, but such a service reduces the net income of the property because of the capital expenditure to provide the parking and the cost of maintenance. There is very little "tax shelter" to be obtained from an investment in free automobile parking for the benefit of tenants. Free parking can increase income, and should be considered when it pays to furnish the service.

Refinance

Refinancing can increase the value of property. There are times when financing can be obtained at a low interest rate and for such a long period for the pay-off that the loan itself is worth a sizable sum of money.

A long-term loan large enough to create "leverage," with a low interest rate, increases "cash flow." Prospective buyers are interested in "cash flow," and will usually pay a higher price for a property with a high "cash flow," showing that refinancing can increase property value.

POINTS TO KEEP IN MIND

√ *A syndicator can increase the value of syndicate owned property by following these procedures:*

√ FOR VACANT LAND OR ACREAGE, the syndicator can subdivide, rezone, improve the land, develop the land, advocate public improvements, explore for natural resources or lease the property.

√ The foregoing suggestions are some of the options open to an imaginative, competent syndicator. There are innumerable methods of increasing the value of vacant land or acreage.

√ FOR INCOME PROPERTY, the syndicator can add improvements, remodel present improvements, advertise to secure new, more aggressive tenants, increase rents, supply automobile parking, or refinance the property.

√ Every parcel of income property poses an individual challenge to the syndicator/manager and to the manager of the syndicate owned real estate.

√ A syndicator is the top level manager for the affairs of his real estate syndicate, and he should explore every avenue and pursue every means to increase the value of income property which is owned by his group.

CHAPTER 17—

The Holding Period

The holding period is the time which elapses between the acquisition of a property and the resale thereof.

A syndicator must give continuing attention to this subject so that his real estate syndicate holds property long enough to make a profit, but not so long that cost of carrying or neighborhood changes diminish the profit.

Acreage or vacant land poses a different problem than improved or income property does.

These are the factors which determine the holding period for syndicated real estate:

For Acreage or Vacant Land:

- Cost of holding property
- Prepaid interest
- Area development
- Subdivision and rezoning
- Sale market

For Income Property:

- The peak of rent income
- Exhaustion of depreciation and equity buildup
- Area development
- Sale market

FOR ACREAGE OR VACANT LAND

Cost of holding property

The cost of holding acreage or vacant land where a syndicator recruits a group of participating investors who are in high income brackets is not possible to compute. Each of the participating investors in the real estate syndicate is in a different income tax bracket, and each of these takes his share of the expense of carrying the property into his personal income tax at whatever rate applies to the top bracket of his tax.

A syndicator must therefore arrive at a carrying cost estimate which would be an average of what the participants might pay. He could assume that half of the cost of carrying the property could be charged against income tax saved by the group.

Thus, a syndicator would assume that his syndicate could carry vacant land or acreage at about half the cost which an individual owner would pay.

Anyone can easily figure that acreage or vacant land which is "leveraged" with a 90 per cent loan at seven per cent interest, real estate taxes of about one per cent of value of the land and miscellaneous expense of about two per cent of land value, would cost approximately 10 per cent of the purchase price to carry the first year. The second year would have the first year's carrying charges added to capital cost, so the second year's expense could be estimated at 11 per cent of land cost. Each year the cost of carrying vacant land increases for an ordinary owner.

A real estate syndicate organized with a group of participating investors who are in high earned income tax brackets can carry and hold land for about half of the cost an individual owner would pay. This would amount to about five per cent of the total cost of the land for the first year.

With this lower holding cost, a real estate syndicate can afford to wait longer for an advantageous opportunity to resell syndicate property, while at the same time converting high income taxes on large earned incomes of participants into long-term capital gain. Five years could be a reasonable holding period for syndicate owned land with interest prepaid.

Prepaid interest

A real estate syndicate which is organized to defer income tax on high ordinary income in certain years and to convert such tax into long-term capital gain must hold the property long enough to use up the prepaid interest.

A syndicate with such objectives usually prepays the interest for a five-year period.

Five years would then be the minimum holding period for land owned by a real estate syndicate interested in prepaid interest and long-term capital gain.

Area development

The pressures of population growth, inflation and other special influences sometimes force prices up so that fantastic profits can be made from the resale of syndicate owned real estate within a very short time because these influences are the basis of rapid area development.

An offer to purchase syndicate owned property at much more than the cost could lead a syndicator to suspect that the prospective buyer has knowledge about the property which is not available to him.

A syndicator should keep fully informed about the value of property under his control, so that a profitable offer can be accepted with confidence even with a short holding period.

Areas can deteriorate. Some unforeseen development, such as the installation of a public garbage dump, a railroad switching yard, or other detrimental neighboring activity could tend to lower values of surrounding property.

Such an unfortunate occurrence would cause an astute manager of a real estate syndicate to revise his ideas about the holding period for property owned by his syndicate in that area.

Immediate resale should be considered for syndicate owned land which is endangered by undesirable development of the area. A short holding period could be the result.

Subdivision and rezoning

Rezoning of agricultural land into residential land suitable for subdivision usually takes the better part of two years time to accomplish. A feasibility study showing support for such a promotion should be made prior to taking any steps toward rezoning syndicate owned land for residential use.

In the event that the feasibility study shows that the project has a reasonable chance of making an acceptable profit, then the holding period would be a minimum of two years in order to work out the rezoning.

Sale market

Every owner of real estate is continuously attempting to gauge the market for property owned. The trend of the market is indicated by the record of transactions, reports of title companies, construction indexes and other sources. These show the present condition of the market and are used to predict the future.

In the last analysis the demand for real estate, and the amount of money which a buyer will pay for certain real estate, pitted against the requirement of the sellers of that type of property, make the market. The daily record of transactions and other statistical information show what has transpired, and indicate the trend for the future.

A syndicator should sell syndicate owned real estate in a market which has not topped out. This means that he must adjust the holding period for such real estate so that the resale of the property occurs while prices are still rising.

Real estate should be offered for sale when it appears that there is a good market for it, and when prices are rising. This offering might be considered as a tentative termination of the holding period, a testing time. An offer of a satisfactory profit on the resale of syndicate real estate, at such a time, and after the syndicator is satisfied that a diligent effort has been made to cover the market for a resale of the property at the asking price, should receive careful consideration. This could be the end of the holding period for that property.

FOR INCOME PROPERTY

The peak of rent income

The basis for valuation of income property is the net income the property produces.

The holding period for income property owned by a real estate syndicate depends to a great degree on the net income which the property can produce when it is rented to the best advantage of the owner.

Any syndicator would try to purchase property such as the 4000 Redbird Boulevard building at the lowest possible price. The price at which this property was purchased produced a net income higher than that which a less astute buyer might have been able to obtain, because he would have paid more for the property.

The 4000 Redbird Boulevard property was actually purchased at a price of $175,000. Based on the income as it was at the time of acquisition, and the expenses as they were then, the property earned a net income of $19,475, or 11.12 per cent on the full purchase price. See Exhibit 11-4, Chapter 11.

The average buyer, satisfied with a 10 per cent return on the building, would have paid $195,000 for it.

The seller was offering the property at a price of $215,000, which would have shown a net return on the full price of nine per cent.

These figures show that there was a spread in the market for this building between the asking price, the average price which might be offered for the property, and the actual purchase price. This is normal in the real estate business.

Exhibit 11-4, Chapter 11, shows this spread in the market, and also reveals that the rents did increase during the next two years, to a point where the net income was $22,100 per annum. A projection of the rent schedule, as shown on Exhibit 11-4, indicates that this would be the peak of rents to be expected until November 30, 1968, at which time the bulk of the existing leases would expire.

A resale of the 4000 Redbird Boulevard property with a net rental of $22,100 would probably produce a capital gain based on a sale price of about $221,000. The buyer would get a ten per cent return on the full price of the property.

The profit to the syndicate would be substantial with a resale of the property at $221,000. In addition to a return of over ten per cent on invested capital, the net proceeds of the sale would produce almost 50 per cent capital gain on the $80,000 invested by the syndicate.

Recall, however, that it was stated that the holding period for income property which is owned by a real estate syndicate depends on the net income which the property can produce when it is rented *to the best advantage of the owner*.

The further projection of net rentals to be expected from the 4000 Redbird property forecasts that the net income of the building could be expected to be at least $28,000 after December 1, 1968, if the leases which expire then are renewed at the prevailing rate obtainable for similar space. Such a rent increase would bring in about $6,000 more net rent per annum. No additional expense would seem to be expected.

The new leases would undoubtedly run for at least five years, and, since other leases overlap the expiring leases, it could be assumed that the gross rents would not increase much for about five years after December 1, 1968.

The holding period for the Redbird Boulevard property would be until December 1, 1968, and any time after that when the market appears to be strong would be a good time to resell the property.

The holding period of four years for this property would have produced a generous income for the members of the syndicate which owned the building. A resale based on a 10 per cent capitalization of the projected $28,000 annual net income could be expected to bring around $280,000 for the property, about $100,000 capital gain on $80,000 invested by the Redbird Boulevard Associates syndicate.

Some part of the depreciation taken in excess of the "straight-line" method would be lost if the property was sold after only four years. The present provisions of the Internal Revenue Code require the recapture of a proportionate share of the excess depreciation taken by accelerated methods of depreciation if the property is not held for ten years.

The 4000 Redbird Boulevard building, with only about 60 per cent of the cost assigned to the building for depreciation purposes, has a relatively small "tax shelter," so the loss of a part of the excess depreciation would be negligible when compared to the handsome capital gain which could be made by a resale of the property.

There are syndicators who would want to keep a property such as the 4000 Redbird Boulevard building for the fine net income which it would produce with the increased rents to be had when the leases expire on November 30, 1968.

Keeping a property which is owned by a real estate syndicate for the rent income to be had is fine, and in this instance, the Redbird Boulevard property would be leased for a period of about five years at the higher rental.

The Redbird Boulevard property is, however, at the approximate peak of net income which can be expected for this five-year period. Expenses, such as real estate taxes, could increase radically, and the rents would only increase as provided in the leases. Actually, the net income could go down during this period, but would still produce a handsome return on the money invested by the syndicate.

I know of one commerical store and office building which was held by a syndicate for about thirty years, during which time the owners took out a tremendous amount of net income. There were a good many lean years during this period when they took out nothing, and really had no equity in the property based on the low rental schedule. Even though the participants had taken out all of the money that they had invested at a time when they refinanced the property, and had, in addition taken out a sum equal to many times their original investment in net income, they still did regret their failure to sell the building when it was at its peak of earning power.

Every income property has an individual holding period which would be best for that particular one. The minimum holding period for the Redbird Boulevard property would appear to be four years.

Exhaustion of depreciation and equity buildup

These two factors which affect the holding period for income property are treated together because the combination of the two influences will inevitably eliminate "tax shelter" within a certain number of years.

To show how this works out, the graph Exhibit 17-1 plots the depreciation and equity buildup on a $100,000 apartment building, assuming a building value of $80,000 for depreciation purposes. The syndicate owner is not the first user of the property.

An assumed remaining life of the building of twenty-five years gives 4 per cent annual straight-line depreciation (salvage value not considered). The declining-balance method of depreciation was used, being 6 per cent of the amount of building value remaining at the end of each year.

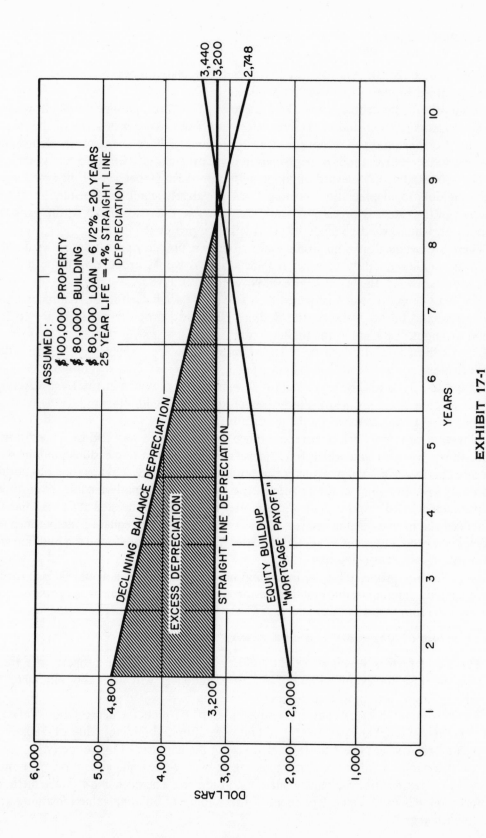

EXHIBIT 17-1

EXAMPLE DEPRECIATION VS EQUITY BUILDUP

Straight-line depreciation is shown on this chart at a constant $3,200 for each year, giving no consideration to salvage value for the sake of simplicity.

The Internal Revenue Code provides that a percentage of accelerated depreciation which would be in excess of straight-line depreciation would be recaptured if the property is sold within ten years after acquisition. This tax provision would recapture a part of the "tax shelter" which the accelerated depreciation had provided in previous years.

The chart Exhibit 17-1 shows the excess depreciation provided by the accelerated depreciation method over the straight-line method. The loss, by recapture of a portion of this excess depreciation, could be an argument for holding income property for a period of at least ten years.

Exhibit 17-1 also shows the annual payments of principal which would be made on an $80,000 loan at 6½ per cent interest, with constant monthly payments of $596.50.

Note that the graph shows depreciation for the first year of $4,800, and a payment of $2,000 on the principal of the loan. "Tax shelter," $4,800, therefore covers all of the net income, which is used to pay the $2,000 on the principal of the loan, and, in addition, covers $2,800 of "cash flow," which is used to pay cash distributions to the participating investors and the syndicators. No income tax would be due in that year on the $4,800, which is the depreciation charged off.

At the end of the eighth year, in this example, the graph shows that the principal payment on the mortgage just about equals the amount charged off for depreciation. From this point on income tax would have to be paid on all of the "cash flow" from this property, and income tax would have to be paid by the participants on some part of the payments on the mortgage after the eighth year of holding the property. This means that the participating investors in this real estate syndicate would thereafter be paying income tax on earnings which they do not receive as cash distributions, earnings which they can only get when the property is sold.

The application of depreciation and the effect of the depletion of accelerated "tax shelter" against increasing principal payments on a mortgage are factors which can determine the holding period for syndicate owned income real estate. The advice of competent tax counsel places these factors in proper perspective so that a syndicator can make a judgment to the benefit of his syndicate.

Area development

The holding period for real estate which is owned by a syndicate should be based in part on the development of the area in which the property is located.

A continuing study of the area surrounding such real estate should be made by the syndicator.

The holding period for such real estate should be timed so that the property is resold while the area is on the upgrade. Waiting to get the last dollar of capital gain risks the peaking out of the neighborhood, and diminishing values for property therein.

The peak of development is usually reached when most of the sizable parcels of land suitable for commercial and apartment use have been improved with buildings. There is a leveling-off of increase in income and value when this point in area development has been reached.

This is the time for terminating the holding period for syndicate-owned income property in the area. When values cease to increase, they usually go down.

Overbuilding of competing income property can depress values of existing property of similar type. Such a situation should cause a syndicator concern, and could terminate the holding period of property controlled by him in that area.

The contemplated installation of undesirable developments in the area near syndicate-owned real estate could cause a syndicator to terminate the holding period for the parcel.

Blight drives out the type of population which has sufficient purchasing power to make an area prosperous. When the improvements in an area surrounding syndicate-owned property become obsolete, and are occupied by a population with low purchasing power, then the prosperity of the area is unfavorably affected. This should cause a syndicator to resell syndicate-controlled property in that area.

Sale market

The sale market for income real estate is constantly changing. A few years ago commercial strip store buildings could be sold in a neighboring city on the basis of an eight per cent return to the buyer on the full price of the property. Now buyers demand at least a ten per cent return, and there are sales made which return a net income to the purchaser of more than ten per cent net on clear buildings.

There is always a spread in the market between what the seller would like to get for his property and what the buyer would like to pay for it.

There are influences which temporarily move the market for income property to higher price levels, and there are others which tend to move it temporarily to lower levels. Two of these influences, for instance, would be inflation and tight money.

A syndicator who had held syndicate owned real estate until he had what he thought to be the peak of income, would take advantage of the influences which made it possible to get a resale of the property in the highest part of the spread of the market, that is, as close as possible to his asking price. An offer which was near this price would then determine the holding period for that property.

POINTS TO KEEP IN MIND

√ It costs money to hold vacant land or acreage. The shortest holding period which will produce a satisfactory long term capital gain is usually the most profitable. Waiting for the last dollar of increase in the resale price often reduces the profit to be made.

√ Prepaid interest deals in vacant land or acreage should usually run long enough to use up the interest which was prepaid when the property was purchased. A shorter holding period would force adjustment of the tax returns of participating investors who used the prepaid interest as income tax deductions in the year in which it was paid.

√ Income property should be held long enough to increase the rents in order to increase the value of the property, or the property should be held until such time as buyers will accept a lower return on invested capital, which also increases the price which can be obtained for the property on resale.

√ Close attention should be paid to the developments in the area in which syndicate owned property is located. Improvement of the area can increase the value of the property, and a deterioration of the area can make property values drop. The holding period for syndicate owned real estate should be terminated if the area starts to deteriorate.

√ Exhaustion of "tax shelter" could be the determining factor in the termination of the holding period for income property. A close watch on this tax saving device should be kept to avoid forcing participating investors to pay income tax on mortgage principal payments, which would, in effect, diminish spendable "cash flow" distributions made to them.

CHAPTER 18—

Determining the Selling Price

When a syndicator decides that the "holding period" is ended, and that syndicate-owned real estate is to be resold, the next step is the determination of the selling price.

The determination of the selling price is complicated by the customary method of doing business when dealing in real estate. To begin with, there is no real marketplace for sale of real estate, such as there is for the sale of stocks and other securities. Then, the seller must decide on an asking price, which is in excess of the price at which an actual sale would be made. The price at which a seller would actually make a deal is the selling price. These two prices must be determined by the seller, without a previous knowledge of what prospective buyers might be willing to pay for such a property.

When the seller, in this case the syndicator, decides on the asking price and the selling price, and when he offers the property for sale in a methodical way in order to get the information about the property into the hands of prospective buyers and real estate brokers, then, hopefully, a market will have been created for the property. At this time the seller can expect to get bids to purchase the property from prospective buyers.

The selling price is the lowest price which the syndicator expects to take in order to make a deal, with hopes that the negotiations with prospective buyers will bring a price close to the asking price.

These are the factors which should be considered and the methods which might be employed to determine the selling price of syndicate-owned real estate.

For Acreage or Vacant Land:

- The appraisal
- Comparison of prices

- The spread of prices
- Charting

For Income Property:

- The appraisal
- Comparison of prices
- The spread of prices
- Capitalization of net income
- Rule of thumb
- Charting

FOR ACREAGE OR VACANT LAND

The appraisal

A competent real estate appraiser can make a valuable contribution to setting the price at which property owned by a real estate syndicate is to be sold.

An active and capable real estate appraiser is constantly comparing property and the prices at which they are being sold. The observant appraiser is also giving consideration to the profitable use of the real estate which is being appraised, and makes recommendations as to the highest and best use of it, as well as a recommendation with regard to the improvements which would produce the most profit for money expended.

An appraiser takes a fresh, objective look at the property which he is employed to value, and which he is comparing with other similar properties which are for sale and which have been sold in the same area.

A large religious order, the owner of substantial real estate holdings in many areas of the country, and the owner of a large parcel of acreage in the booming development fringe of a city near Los Angeles, had an appraisal made of the value of their property at least once each year. The property, which they would have sold for about $1,700 per acre about ten years ago, is now valued at about $5,000 per acre or more.

The owner chose a different appraiser each time, thus obtaining a fresh approach, together with new supporting data and a different viewpoint as to the highest and best use of the land.

This procedure kept the real estate committee and the real estate manager of the owning organization in touch with latest developments in the area, and with current sale prices at very little cost. The tract, of approximately 200 acres, is now valued at approximately $1,000,000, against a value of about $340,000 about ten years ago.

A real estate appraisal can be obtained from a competent, well-qualified appraiser for a relatively reasonable fee, an expenditure well made to help in determining the selling price of property owned by a real estate syndicate.

Comparison of prices

The syndicator who is keeping a close check on the transactions in real estate in the area of the property which is owned by his syndicate has a continuing appraisal of the property going for him. He should at all times be shopping to buy property for another syndicate which might be organized. This gives him the pulse of the market for real estate similar to the property which is for sale by his syndicate.

A record of transactions which involve comparable property, and similar property in smaller tracts or parcels which are sold in the neighborhood of syndicate owned land, should be kept, with dates of such sales.

Particular attention should be paid to the zoning of the other parcels which are sold in the area. There is a big difference in the price of raw land and of land which is zoned for a more intensive use. A real estate syndicate which merely holds land for a rise in price would expect to get a smaller capital gain than would be possible if the land had become ripe for development and had been tentatively rezoned for subdivision into small parcels, while being held.

The comparison of the prices of land offered for sale against the actual sale prices given in the daily record of transactions gives a syndicator a good idea of the spread between asking and selling prices. The bid prices are difficult to uncover.

Comparison of asking prices and selling prices is one of the best ways to determine the selling price of real estate owned by a real estate syndicate.

The spread of prices

The comparison of prices focuses attention on the spread of prices between the asking and the selling price of property. An aggressive sales campaign can sometimes produce a sale between the two prices, which results in more profit for the real estate syndicate.

In determining the selling price for syndicate-owned real estate, a syndicator should try to support a price which is in the highest range of the spread of market prices.

The asking price should be high enough to allow some flexibility for negotiating, with possibility of obtaining a sale at a price higher than the average selling price, or minimum acceptable price. It is accepted practice to ask more for real estate than the rock-bottom price. For instance, the seller might be asked to provide financing, instead of being offered an all-cash deal. This requirement might cause a seller to hold to his asking price to compensate for the terms which would be granted.

There are situations, such as those where a tax problem is pressing a buyer to make a quick purchase of real estate, which forces a buyer to pay more for real estate than he would if time allowed for more leisurely negotiating. Such a situation can bring more profit from the sale of syndicate-owned property.

Give consideration to the spread of prices when determining the asking price and the selling price of syndicate-owned real estate. Aim high!

Charting

The record of asking prices and sale prices of properties which has been compiled by a syndicator to keep abreast of the market for property of similar character to that owned by his syndicate can be plotted on a graph. Use unit prices, such as the price per acre, and plot these on a graph showing the time of the sale. Key the entry with a letter or number so that it can be identified against the record of the sale. See Exhibit 11-3, Chapter 11, for a sample. Show the trend of prices by drawing a curve through the plot points on the graph.

A syndicator who charts the market for real estate which is of interest to him has a quick, ready reference to use when determining the selling price of land owned by his syndicate. Asking prices can also be plotted to show the spread between asking and selling prices of similar property. Such a chart gives a syndicator a solid knowledge of the trend of prices of property similar in character to the syndicate property to be sold.

Many syndicators depend heavily on charting, because it not only provides an easy way to keep abreast of the market, but it shows the trend and helps to determine the holding period and the selling price of syndicate owned real estate.

FOR INCOME PROPERTY

The appraisal

The appraisal of syndicate-owned income property provides all of the advantages which would apply to appraisal of acreage and vacant land when used to determine the selling price.

A real estate appraisal of income property usually provides a comparison of rents which prevail in the area of appraised property to support the findings of value. The net income which is being earned, figured against the rents which prevail, provides the basis for computation of value by the economic or capitalization method.

An appraiser also values the property by estimating the value of the land and figuring the reproduction cost of the improvements.

A real estate appraisal has value for income tax purposes, to check insurance coverage, and would be a great help in the determination of the selling price of syndicate owned income property.

Comparison of prices

A comparison of prices, made in the same manner as would be made for acreage or vacant land, has some place in determining the value of syndicate owned real estate. Much detailed information is needed to make a real comparison of income properties in order to arrive at fair comparisons.

A syndicator who continuously keeps in touch with the market for income properties by shopping for additional buildings suitable for further syndications can form a judgment of the market, which is valuable in determining the selling price of property to be resold.

An active syndicator who *tests* the market by making offers to purchase income property for the purpose of forming other real estate syndicates can get a real feel of both the asking and selling prices which prevail. A syndicator with this kind of experience usually has no difficulty in determining the asking and selling prices of real estate already owned by his syndicate.

The spread of prices

There is the same sort of spread to be found between the asking and selling prices of income property as is to be found with land prices.

A syndicator must get to know what this spread is, so that he can determine the asking and selling prices for his syndicate property when it is to be resold. The spread of the market is gauged by shopping around for real estate which is comparable to the property which is to be priced.

The asking price for syndicate-owned income property should be set so that it is in the highest bracket of the spread of the market so that there is some room for negotiating when an interested buyer is found. The objective is to arrive at a selling price which is above the figure which was set as a minimum acceptable price, and as close to the asking price as the buyer will go.

Capitalization of net income

The capitalization of net income is one of the best ways of determining the selling price of income property.

This method is recognized as the one most likely to be used to determine the asking and selling prices of income property.

A few years ago income property could be sold on the basis of an 8 per cent return on the full price of an attractive, well-located and rented strip commercial building. Now the buyers expect to get 10 per cent or more as a net return on a clear building of similar type.

A shrewd syndicator, finding that this is the situation, would capitalize his net income from syndicate-owned income property on the basis of a 10 per cent return on the full price as computed. This price would be used as the selling price, the base line for the spread of prices, of which a higher asking price would be the top of the market spread.

A syndicator who has managed to increase rents of an income property, without increasing expenses of operation, will therefore be able to set the selling price up $10 for each $1 of annual rent increase obtained. An increase of $25 per month, obtained from each of ten tenants, would bring in an extra $3,000 per annum, which would increase the selling price by $30,000.

There should always be a spread between the selling price and the asking price of real estate. The spread could be based on an asking price established by capitalizing the net income to return 9 per cent on the full price of the property to be sold.

A keen syndicator makes a real effort to find a buyer who will pay a price for syndicate-owned property which is close to the asking price. There are buyers who will pay more for a particular property, or perhaps a favored location. Income tax situations sometimes force a buyer to pay more in order to get a quick deal.

A syndicator who has acquired a solid sense of values by comparing prices of income properties similar to the syndicate-owned real estate will set the minimum acceptable price, the selling price, in alignment with the current market, and will try to get a higher price by offering to sell at a higher figure.

Rule of thumb

One rule of thumb which is used to gauge value of income real estate is based on a determination of the number of times the gross annual rent must be multiplied to match the price of the property.

This is a rough estimate of value, but comparison of the 2800 E. Main Street property, used as an example in the prospectus, Chapter 8, against the 4000 Redbird Boulevard building, described in Exhibit 10-4, Chapter 10, reveals the remarkable accuracy of this method when the two are examined with the same multiple of gross rents.

The East Main Street property was priced at 8 x the $21,600 gross annual rental for a 9.7 per cent net return on the full price of $175,000.

The 4000 Redbird Boulevard building was priced at 7.3 x the gross annual rental of $23,880, for an 11.12 per cent return on the full price of $175,000. The Redbird Boulevard building was a good buy at this price, as the continued comparison of the two properties demonstrates.

Suppose that the Redbird property had been priced at 8 x the gross annual rental of $23,880. In that event the price of the property would have been about $190,000. The net income—$19,475—would have been just a little over 10 per cent net return on the $190,000 price, very close to the 9.7 per cent return on the East Main Street property at 8 x the gross rent of $21,600.

Many prospective buyers and real estate brokers use a "rule of thumb" approach to valuing property. They quickly divide the price of the property by the annual rent and then decide if they have any interest in the property as compared to other properties offered in the same market.

Some properties have higher expenses than others do, and some properties which are offered for sale are under-rented. Such situations could make a "rule of thumb" approach very inaccurate.

Every syndicator who has syndicate-owned property to sell encounters prospective buyers who use the "rule of thumb" approach to valuation of property. This method is a very rough method of valuation, and if the property being offered has low expenses and a high net return on the full price, a syndicator selling syndicated-owned income real estate should be prepared to point out that the net income earned on the full price of the property is the best gauge of value.

Charting

Exhibit 11-4, Chapter 11, shows graphically the projection of rents for the 4000 Redbird Boulevard property. When the time comes to sell this syndicate-owned income property, then the rents should be approximately as forecasted.

Suppose, now, that the rents for this building have been increased to $33,000, and the net income is at the rate of $28,000 per annum.

If the average buyer might pay a price which would produce 10 per cent on the full price paid, he would be willing to pay $280,000 for the Redbird Boulevard building.

A syndicator who charts to determine the selling price of income property must have knowledge of the market for that type of property, since it is obvious that a market in which buyers would accept a 9 per cent return would chart out to a $310,000 selling price for the same property.

Charting is the easiest and most reliable way to work out the selling price of income property, and to show the progress which has been made by the syndicate during the holding period. It is a device to be used in connection with the particular building owned by the real estate syndicate. A separate chart would be needed for every building which was to be valued by this method.

The chart shows the price at which the building could be sold to produce the same percentage net return which the property produced when it was bought by the syndicate, the average price which purchasers might be willing to pay, and the asking price which a seller would offer to sell at.

The "selling Price Chart" is not a device to use to convince buyers that the property is a good buy. The chart is strictly a seller's guide.

The graph, Exhibit 11-4, Chapter 11, indicates that the 4000 Redbird Boulevard property should be offered for sale at an asking price of about $310,000. The selling price should be determined at not much less than $280,000 when increased rents and net income are obtained as forecast in the projection.

POINTS TO KEEP IN MIND

√ Determining the selling price of syndicate owned real estate is a matter of comparisons and judgment.

√ Real estate appraisals have real value as a support for the judgment of a syndicator seeking to determine the selling price of syndicate owned real estate.

√ Shopping the market for property which is similar to the property to be sold is a good way to establish the going asking prices for such property.

√ Mortgage lenders keep close tab on real estate values and an opinion of value from their appraisers can be most helpful to a syndicator.

√ Trend indicators, such as dollar volume of deeds, and individual recordings or news items concerning sales of comparable property should not be overlooked by a syndicator when he is pricing syndicate owned property for resale.

√ Construction costs indicate the replacement value of improvements, and, coupled with the cost of similar vacant land, could influence the price at which syndicate owned property should be resold.

CHAPTER 19—

The Selling Campaign

The sale of syndicate-owned property at a profit when the holding period is ended is the ultimate goal of the syndicator. This step, when successfully achieved, produces the capital gain which is the only goal of a real estate syndication which involves acreage or vacant land. The profitable resale of syndicate-owned income property is the crowning achievement which concludes the operation which has produced a handsome net income during the holding period.

A profitable resale of syndicate property sets the stage for the formation of another syndicate, using the same satisfied participating investors. A syndicator who has such a group of investors has the best endorsement of his competence and judgment to aid him in recruiting additional participants in his future ventures.

Communications are the main obstacles to the sale of real estate. Finding prospective purchasers of real estate is not an easy task. Every means of communication available should be used to present information about property to be sold to those who can assist in the sale, and to prospective buyers by direct contact.

There simply is no organized market for the sale of real estate which is comparable to the markets for the sale of stocks and other securities. Prospective buyers for larger parcels of real estate are particularly difficult to contact.

A syndicator, even one who is in the real estate business, must create his own market for property which he wishes to sell. It is his job to provide the selling material, to arouse the interest of prospective buyers, and of those who can assist in the sale of the property, such as real estate brokers, lawyers, accountants and others.

These are the tools which are needed, the actions to take, and the contacts to make to resell real estate owned by a syndicate.

For Acreage or Vacant Land

- Descriptive data
- Advertising

• Real estate brokers

For Income Property

• Descriptive data
• Advertising
• Real estate brokers

FOR ACREAGE OR VACANT LAND

Descriptive data

I will use the Old Ranch property as the example for the preparation of descriptive matter for use in the resale of acreage by a syndicator.

Assume that the Old Ranch Partnership has held the land for three years, during which time tentative rezoning into half-acre lots has been gained. The water and sewer mains have been extended to serve the property when needed. Determination of the offering prices and minimum selling prices have been made.

Selling material will be needed, and the syndicator should prepare a description of the property and a plot plan. Legal descriptions of the entire property and of the seven smaller parcels which can be sold should be obtained. Pictures, including the property, the views to be seen from the site, and the surrounding land and improvements, are necessary. A topographical map, survey, map of tentative subdivision tracts, soil tests and other information should be available.

Local chambers of commerce usually have free maps of the locality, with well-thought-out promotional material. Utility companies also are good sources of such material.

The material which is assembled should be sufficient for any larger use, such as a direct mailing, and there should be enough on hand to supply ordinary demand for it.

I have made good use of a relatively low-priced copy machine for reproducing plats and form letters in smaller quantities. These, and property descriptions, are subject to changes which make the printing of large quantities wasteful.

The description of the Old Ranch, shown as Exhibit 19-1, is an example of the type of material needed by the syndicator to send to parties who might be interested in purchasing the property. Such a description can be mailed to residential developers, real estate brokers and investors who might want to continue to hold the land for tax purposes and further appreciation in price.

This type of property description gives much of the information needed to stimulate the interest of prospects to a point where more detailed information is required.

The plot plan can be simple, such as the one shown as Exhibit 19-2. This plot plan was made from a zoning map, enlarged to fit on $8\frac{1}{2}'' \times 11''$ paper.

A syndicator would have a small plot plan and available copies made by the engineer who laid out the subdivisions.

I have found that a limited amount of engineering information, such as the spot elevations, and perhaps a small diagram of a subdivision, add interest to a plot plan. More details clutter up such a plot plan, which is to be used to attract a prospective buyer so that he asks for the more detailed drawings.

EXHIBIT 19-1

THE OLD RANCH
200 ACRES
RIPE FOR RESIDENTIAL SUBDIVISION

LOCATION :   Located about two miles west of Fandango, California, the "Old Ranch" consists of 200 acres of rolling land. There is 3,000' of frontage on Seaside Road, with average depth of 3,000' to the Pacific Ocean. There is a sand beach, above which the land has an average 14' of elevation which forms a bluff along the beach. The parcel has an elevation of 12' above sea level at the southeast corner, rising to about 37' at the northwest corner.

FEATURES :   The gentle, rolling contour of the land provides splendid marine views. There are fine mountain views to the north. A new branch of the state university is a short distance away, and a new light industrial park within two miles. Sewer and water mains are along the entire Seaside Road frontage. This land is ripe for residential subdivision.

ZONING :   Present zoning is for agriculture and the right to drill for oil, gas and minerals. Adjacent land is similarly zoned. Oil activity and right of surface entry were abandoned some years ago. Tentative approval of residential one-half acre lots has been granted for the entire 200 acres. Engineering has been done to lay out approximately 400 lots of one-half acre each, with an interesting street pattern. The design allows for division into seven tracts.

RESTRICTIONS :   All residences in the various tracts are to be constructed to meet the specifications of the seller as to size, style and quality of workmanship, unless the entire 200 acres is purchased by one party. Streets, curbs, gutters and street lighting shall meet county requirements. All electric service is to be underground.

ENTIRE
  PROPERTY :   The entire "Old Ranch" property, consisting of 200 acres, is for sale at a price of $5,500 per acre, or a total purchase price of $1,100,000. The seller will contract to sell at this price with partial payments down and annually, interest to be at 7% per annum on the unpaid balance. The smaller tracts can be taken out by making payment of the balance of purchase price on said parcel. Takeout parcels shall be first taken from Seaside Road, with ocean frontage tracts taken for development last.

TRACTS :   The seven smaller tracts range in size from about 23 acres to 30 acres each. Parcels 1 and 2, as shown on plot plan, are typical of these tracts. Parcel No. 1 is priced at about $6,500 per acre, at a total price of $150,000. Other prices and tract maps on request.

BROKERS :   Broker cooperation is solicited.

OLD RANCH PARTNERSHIP, Owner

P. O. Box 7777, Fandango, Calif.   Phone 777-88-4444

EXHIBIT 19-2

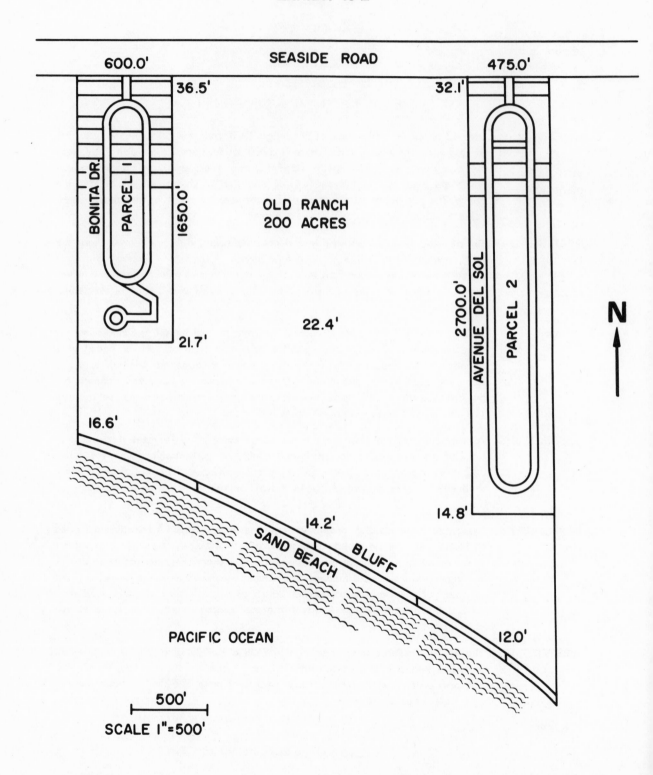

Legal descriptions of the entire parcel, that is, the Old Ranch property, and of the smaller subdivision tracts should be available; the engineer can furnish these.

Pictures of vacant land are usually not great selling aids, but they are necessary. They should be taken by an experienced photographer under the direction of the syndicator. Views which can be seen from various points on the subject property usually contribute more than pictures of the property itself. An aerial picture is good to have if it shows anything of interest.

Aerial photos are usually available from a local aerial photographer for a reasonable price, if the activity in the area justifies a coverage of it. Pictures of nearby public improvements can usually be obtained free from the local chamber of commerce.

A topographical map will be a part of the work of the engineer who lays out the subdivisions. Prints should be available for the inspection of prospective buyers. Subdivision maps and prints of surveys should likewise be made available to prospects, so that developers can work out plans for improvements.

Maps of the community, often to be had free or for a small charge from the chamber of commerce, should indicate the location of the property and of other points of interest to a prospective buyer.

Advertising

Advertising to promote the sale of syndicate acreage or vacant land can be done in many ways and in a number of mediums.

Newspapers and financial and builder publications about cover the field for this type of advertising, but "For Sale" signs on the property are effective, and direct mail advertising cannot be overlooked.

A syndicator should consider contacting a few developers to find out which medium attracts them when they are interested in acquiring land, so that no avenue of contact will be overlooked in presenting the land "for sale."

The sale of acreage is a specialized business. The problem is to reach parties who would be interested in buying acreage for development, or to hold for further capital appreciation.

Advertising in the local or metropolitan newspapers always appears to be the easiest way to attract prospective buyers, and should be the first method to try. Advertisements do not need to be large, but they should contain enough information to bring responses from interested prospects.

Advertising in financial papers can reach prospects who are in high income brackets, and who might be interested in holding the land for a longer period to save earned income taxes and to convert the tax savings into capital gains.

Builder publications list the new projects in an area, and record building permits and real estate transfers. Advertising in such a publication can produce satisfactory results.

Painted "For Sale" signs installed on the property can produce interest from prospective buyers who scout the area. These signs should be large enough to be readable from a passing car, but not billboard size.

Direct mail advertising can be rewarding. The mailing list can be taken from the telephone book, the advertisers in the real estate sections of metropolitan newspapers, and from classified advertisers. Direct mail advertising must be informative and attractive. Coverage of every real estate firm, lawyer, accountant, subdivider and the business managers of motion picture or television personalities can usually be handled with 1,000 to 2,000 mailing pieces.

Real estate brokers

Real estate brokers provide one of the best chances for the sale of acreage. They do answer newspaper advertisements, but they respond best to direct mail advertising. A coverage of all of the real estate brokers within a reasonable radius of the subject property is well worth while. The radius could be up to 100 miles in all directions. A description of the property for sale, together with a small plat, and a letter which states that the property is available at a certain asking price, attracts attention. A statement of the commission to be paid to a selling broker excites interest and avoids any misunderstanding about this important subject.

Some development companies have their own brokers and will not deal directly with a seller. They expect their broker to screen the properties offered and to obtain all pertinent information for them, for which their broker expects to be paid a commission if a sale results.

Repeat coverage of real estate brokers is mandatory. I have found that communications are poor in the real estate business. Large real estate companies do not always pass open listings to all of their salesmen. I know that this is true because I have had salesmen inquire about properties which had "For Sale" signs on them. The same properties had been previously listed with the main office of the same company. I conclude that it is wise to cover all branch offices of large real estate firms.

A repeat of coverage of real estate brokers should be made every three months or so, to keep them alert to the listing.

FOR INCOME PROPERTY

Descriptive data

The 4000 Redbird Boulevard property is used here as an example for the preparation of descriptive matter to be used in the resale of income property by a syndicator.

Assume that the Redbird Boulevard Associates have held the property for a period of a little over four years, during which time they have enjoyed a fine return on money invested.

Now the majority of the leases which would expire on November 30, 1968, are presumed to have been renewed at rents then prevailing, with some tenant changes.

The asking price and the selling price have both been determined by the syndicator.

The data which would be essential for the presentation of the Redbird Boulevard property for resale would consist of the following items: a description of the property, a plot plan showing the property, the surrounding improvements and tenants; a legal description of the real estate for sale, a print of survey, an aerial picture of the area, pictures of the building and surrounding improvements, in color.

Maps of the locality can be obtained from the local chamber of commerce, on which the site of the property can be indicated.

The description of the 4000 Redbird Boulevard property, Exhibit 19-3, gives most of the information which would be required to interest a prospective buyer. Such a description should be carefully prepared, because this is the main selling tool to be used by the syndicator.

EXHIBIT 19-3

PRIME COMMERCIAL BUILDING

4000 REDBIRD BOULEVARD

Fandango, California

LAND: 160 feet on Redbird Boulevard, running through to Hale Avenue, with a depth of 200 feet. ZONED C-2.

BUILDING: Nearly new, well constructed store building, one story high, containing 8 stores. Exterior, rear and side walls of concrete blocks; fronts of plate glass and aluminum with glass louvres above. Steel beam construction allows development of all-sized stores.

LOCATION: Fandango is a City of about 65,000, in Ventura County, California. It is predicted that the County will have 1,000,000 population by 1980, with 500,000 in the Fandango area. Traffic count at this point is at 38,000 cars per day on the fourlane artery. The property is in the area of two well established shopping centers containing two branch banks and a branch of a large federal saving and loan association.

PARKING: Four rows of off street parking across the entire front of the property, space for 50 cars. Tenant parking and deliveries on the 20' strip across rear of property.

INCOME:

4000—Clipper Club	6% of sales vs	$ 500.00	to 7/4/74
4002—Barber	average	200.00	to 11/30/73
4004—Beauty Salon	"	350.00	to 11/30/73
4006—Auto Finance	"	300.00	to 11/30/73
4008—Health Food	"	350.00	to 11/30/73
4010—Real Estate	"	350.00	to 11/30/73
4012—Dry Cleaner	"	350.00	to 11/30/73
4016—Television	4% of sales vs	350.00	to 2/14/72
TOTAL MONTHLY RENT		$2,750.00	

TOTAL ANNUAL RENT $33,000.00

EXPENSES:

(Estimated)	General taxes	$3,500.00	
	Insurance	700.00	
	Parking lighting	300.00	
	Parking maintenance	300.00	
	Repairs & miscellaneous	200.00	$ 5,000.00

NET INCOME BEFORE MORTGAGE REQUIREMENTS $28,000.00

TRUST DEED: First Trust Deed—Amerado, Inc., originally
$110,000, balance $92,620 payable $756
per month, $5\frac{1}{2}\%$, Due 9/1/83—Annual interest (approx) $ 5,000.00

NET INCOME ON EQUITY, (10.7% on $217,400)   " $23,000.00

Paid on Principal, Annual   " $ 4,000.00

NET SPENDABLE, "Cash Flow"—8.7% on equity $19,000.00

PRICE: $310,000   JOHN J. JONES, REAL ESTATE
22 "A" Street, Ventura, California

EXHIBIT 19-3 (CONTINUED)

The plot plan, Exhibit 19-4, shows the streets, the surrounding improvements and the subject property, with dimensions. Such plot plans can be obtained from title companies or county assessors, and, with tenant names inserted, reproductions can be made available.

A print of survey, on which the legal description is detailed, should be available for inspection.

Aerial pictures are obtainable for most active communities at reasonable prices. One print is sufficient for the inspection of prospective buyers.

Pictures of the property are effective and impressive. The improvements surrounding the subject property are important because they form the background of neighboring attractions and the occupants of the residential buildings comprise the community of purchasers who support the stores.

In recent years I have taken my own pictures of property. Enlargements of 35 millimeter slides to 5″ × 7″ color prints make a good impression. Enlargements of color prints made by inexpensive cameras do a good job. Taking a number of pictures at various times of the day and with different lighting and traffic conditions makes it possible to select the best ones for enlargement. Overlapping pictures taken from the same distance away from a long, low building can be stripped together to make a good showing. A selection of colored pictures, enlarged to a reasonable size, mounted on Bristol board and covered with transparent plastic sheet, makes an impression which is invaluable.

These are the descriptive tools needed to submit the syndicate income property for resale. The quantity of each can be limited to immediate needs, with a supply on hand at all times to give out to interested prospects.

Advertising

Newspapers, financial publications, real estate trade papers, "For Sale" signs, direct mail, all can be great if they produce buyers.

"For Sale" signs on the property undoubtedly produce the best results for dollars expended. Such signs do appear to be out of place on improved property, however.

Classified advertising should be carefully prepared so that the message is clear, and the size of the advertisement relative to that of other property of similar characteristics.

The message which is to be conveyed for the Redbird property is that it is "For Sale." Under this classification the property should be very briefly described, with some eye-catching statement included, together with the name, address and phone number of one who can give further information. In larger papers, the advertisements are smaller.

Real estate advertising is used only to attract prospective buyers to the party who wants to sell the property. The seller then does the rest of the job.

Real estate brokers

Real estate brokers are usually highly interested in getting listings on commercial or income property.

This type of property usually sells for a price high enough to bring large commissions, and the seller is usually businesslike in the furnishing of accurate information about the property. Prospective buyers recognize profit opportunities and have the ability to analyze factual data.

A submission of an income property "For Sale" to a real estate broker should be handled in a uniform manner which includes a letter of submission, briefly stating the facts concerning the sale, and the commission arrangement. A descriptive statement should accompany the letter.

A broker really interested in working on the property will have some questions, and will make inquiries.

The asking price should be kept absolutely the same for all brokers, and they should be notified of any change in price promptly. Any indication that offers will be considered should be accompanied by a statement that such offers must be in writing, supported by an earnest money deposit, in order to receive consideration.

POINTS TO KEEP IN MIND

√ A "selling campaign" is a merchandising campaign.

√ A syndicator, seeking to resell syndicate owned property at a profit must merchandise the property.

√ The syndicator must overcome the "lack of communications" which is one of the problems of merchandising real estate.

EXHIBIT 19-4

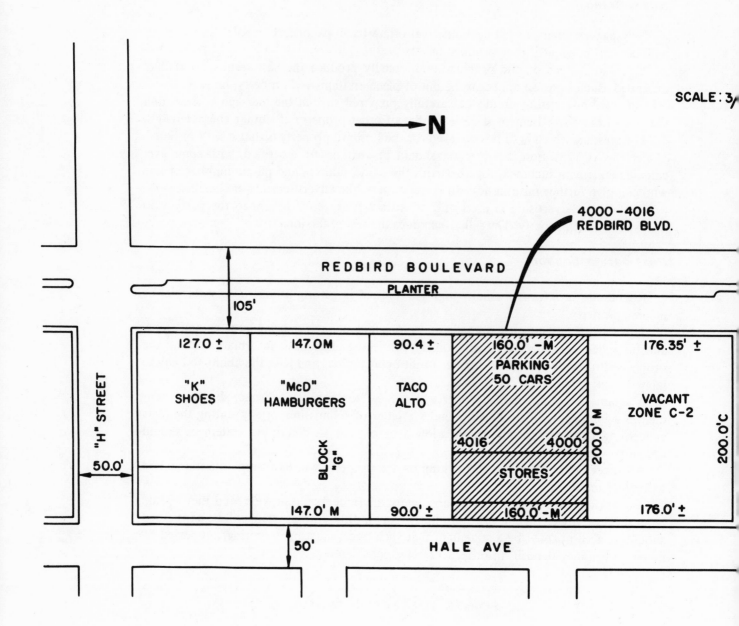

SCALE: 3/

EXHIBIT 19-4 (CONTINUED)

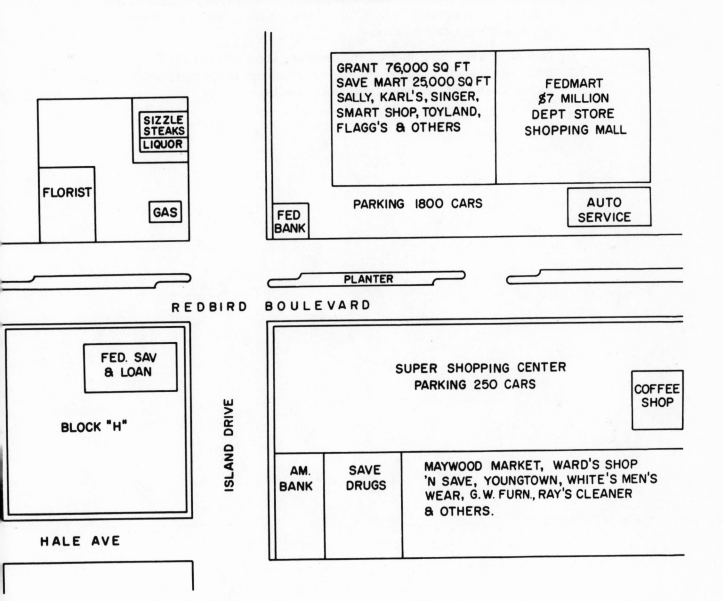

√ "Lack of communications" can be overcome by furnishing pertinent factual material and arguments in favor of purchasing the property to prospective buyers and real estate brokers.

√ Newspaper advertising, direct mail advertising and signboard advertising, all contribute towards supplying the "communications" which make a satisfactory resale of syndicate owned real estate possible.

CHAPTER 20—

Dividing the Profits

Dividing the profits of a successful real estate syndication is the pleasant procedure which marks the achievement of the goal of the syndicator. The payment to the participating investors of their share of the profit firmly establishes in their minds that they made a sound financial move when they placed confidence in the syndicator's capability and integrity by investing in his real estate syndicate.

The division of the profits of a real estate syndication is complicated, however, by the income tax problems, the arrangements for compensation of the syndicator, and the devices used in the organizational agreement to minimize his income tax.

The two main types of real estate, acreage and vacant land, and income property, present different problems to a syndicator when dividing the profits, but the steps to be taken for the division of profits of both types are the same.

When a satisfactory deal has been made for the resale of syndicate owned real estate, the procedure for dividing the profits is as follows:

For All Types of Syndicate-Owned Real Estate:

- Complete all syndicate transactions
- Review the organizational agreement with accountant
- Obtain escrow closing statements
- Prepare records and documents for closing out organization
- Prepare reports for syndicate members
- Prepare tax return for syndicate
- Pay out all funds according to syndicate agreement and dissolve organization

FOR ACREAGE OR VACANT LAND

Complete all syndicate transactions

When a resale is worked out for syndicate real estate, the deal closing usually takes from thirty to sixty days, and an experienced syndicator would inform his group that such a time would elapse before funds would be available for distribution. The time is needed, of course, to complete the title work, get the documents, and to allow the purchaser to arrange for the funds to close the transaction.

Such notice by a syndicator to his syndicate group avoids any problems which might arise because the investors are eager to get their money and profit out of the proceeds of the sale, and are impatient with delays.

The time during which the deal is being closed should be used by the syndicator to complete all transactions of the syndicate by the payment of all of the obligations of the syndicate. He should get a solid commitment from the syndicate accountant and attorney as to their charges, so that their bills can be paid and a prompt distribution of the proceeds of the sale can be made.

The completion of syndicate transactions includes the deal closing, the distribution of the proceeds of the sale and the dissolution of the syndicate organization.

The syndicator, the syndicate accountant and attorney should work together to complete the syndicate transactions.

One method of working out the closing details of a real estate syndicate would be to hold all funds in escrow until all bills have been paid and then distributing the cash proceeds of the sale to the participants in the syndicate.

Another method would be promptly to distribute all but a small portion of the proceeds of sale, holding back enough to cover the final expenses expected.

I have found that the second method works best. The final accounting of the small balance which has been retained can then be accompanied by a full report of the transaction, a copy of the syndicate income tax return, and a check for the small cash balance due.

Review the organizational agreement with accountant

The syndicator, the syndicate accountant, and probably the attorney should re-examine the syndicate agreement so that the distribution of the proceeds of sale of syndicate property is made as provided in the agreement.

Obtain escrow closing statements

A copy of the escrow closing statement should be furnished to every participant in a real estate syndicate.

Prepare accounting records for closing out organization

The syndicator should arrange for the syndicate accountant to get the accounting records in shape for closing out the organization when the time for dissolution arrives.

Prepare reports for syndicate members

Syndicate investors expect to get reports which explain and supplement the usual accounting reports and tax returns.

Exhibits 20-1, 20-2, and 20-3 are examples of the kind of reports which could be used in connection with an acreage syndicate and which show the whole picture of the transactions of the Old Ranch Partnership, which has been used as an example of an acreage syndication.

Exhibit 20-1 was set up to show that the property was sold at a price which would produce a profit of $500,000. Expenses of sale are not shown, to simplify the exhibit.

This example was taken from an almost identical deal in which the profit was more than that assumed for the Old Ranch deal.

Note the expenses of $118,500, which the Limited Partners were able to charge off against high earned income and which were converted to low-taxed capital gain by this deal.

EXHIBIT 20-1

OLD RANCH PARTNERSHIP

DISTRIBUTION OF PROCEEDS OF SALE OF "OLD RANCH"

NET PROCEEDS OF SALE OF "OLD RANCH"—(after expenses of sale)		$1,027,000
Payment of balance of Purchase Price	$350,000	
Repayment of Limited Partners' investment	177,000	(527,000)
TOTAL TAXABLE CAPITAL GAIN		$ 500,000
EXPENSES OF OPERATION—3 years:		
Interest	$ 84,000	
Organizational expense	3,000	
Taxes	9,000	
Management	22,500	
Repayment of expenses advanced by Limited Partners—total		($ 118,500*)
TOTAL CASH TO BE DISTRIBUTED		$ 381,500
Pay to Limited Partners 80% of $381,500 =		(305,200)
Pay to General Partners 20% of $381,500 =		($ 76,300)
		–0–

*This $118,500, contributed by Limited Partners for expenses of holding "Old Ranch" for 3 years, was charged by them against their ordinary incomes, assumed to be in the 50% average income tax bracket. Limited Partners would pay long term income tax on their shares of this amount. This is a demonstration of the conversion of high earned income into long term capital gain to make an effective saving of income tax.

Exhibit 20-2 shows the timing of the investment by a single limited partner over the three-year holding period, the repayment of the amounts which he invested, and his share of the limited partners' portion of the profit from the resale of the Old Ranch property.

EXHIBIT 20-2

OLD RANCH PARTNERSHIP

Statement of Investment and Profit
of Individual Limited Partners

LIMITED PARTNER CONTRIBUTIONS

	Capital Investment	Expense of Operation	Total
First Year:			
Down payment plus improvements	$ 7,700		
Expenses		$ 7,300	
TOTAL 1ST YEAR CONTRIBUTION			$15,000
Second Year:			
Principal installment	$ 5,000		
Expenses		$ 3,500	
TOTAL 2ND YEAR CONTRIBUTION			$ 8,500
Third Year:			
Principal installment	$ 5,000		
Expenses		$ 1,050	
TOTAL 3RD YEAR CONTRIBUTION			$ 6,050
TOTAL CONTRIBUTIONS FOR 3 YEAR PERIOD	$17,700	$11,850	$29,550
DISTRIBUTION OF PROCEEDS OF SALE			
Repayment of capital investment	($17,700)		
Repayment of expenses advanced		($11,850)*	
Payment of 10% of balance proceeds of sale		($30,520)**	
Total taxable as long term gain		$42,370	

*10% of $118,500—See note on Exhibit 20-1.
**Individual partner's share of $305,000 gain

Exhibit 20-3, a Statement of Earnings and Profit of General Partners, shows the profit which would be made by the syndicator or syndicators, the total of the management fee for the three-year holding period, and the potential earning of sale commissions which might be made if the syndicator, or one of them, was a real estate broker.

Such a report would only be of interest to the syndicators, in this case the general partners.

EXHIBIT 20-3

OLD RANCH PARTNERSHIP

STATEMENT OF EARNINGS AND PROFIT

OF GENERAL PARTNERS

Long term capital gain 20% × $381,500	$ 76,300
Ordinary income—management fee—3 years @ $7,500	22,500
Total profit and earnings of general partners	98,800
NOTE: A syndicator who was the general partner in an acreage syndicate, and was also in the real estate business could expect to participate in brokerage commissions estimated at	37,500
Total profit and earnings for syndicator/broker	$136,300

Prepare tax returns for syndicate members

The syndicator should see to the preparation of syndicate income tax returns by the syndicate accountant, to be sent to the participants in the deal with the final closing payment of the proceeds of sale of the property.

Pay out all funds according to syndicate agreement and then dissolve organization

A real estate syndicate is organized for a one-time deal, and when the syndicate property is resold, the syndicator, with the advice and assistance of the syndicate accountant and attorney, closes out the bank account of the organization, distributes all funds in accordance with the provisions of the syndicate agreement, and dissolves the organization.

FOR INCOME PROPERTY

Complete all syndicate transactions

For income property, the procedure is the same as for acreage, with the addition of the closeout of the operation of the property. The syndicate accountant picks up the operational items which were prorated in the escrow closing statement, so that they are transferred for proper tax handling.

Review of organizational agreement with accountant

This procedure would be the same as it would have been with an acreage deal.

Secure escrow closing statements

Same as with acreage deal.

Prepare accounting records for closing out organization

This accounting procedure would parallel the acreage work, except that the operation of the property would have to be accounted for.

Prepare reports for syndicate members

Exhibits 20-4 through 20-14 show some of the ways in which the syndicate transactions can be reported for the benefit of the participating investors and of the syndicators.

EXHIBIT 20-4

4000 REDBIRD BOULEVARD ASSOCIATES

DISTRIBUTION OF PROCEEDS OF SALE

	Limited Partners	General Partners	
Cash proceeds of sale (after expenses & prorations)			$182,380
DISTRIBUTION OF CASH			
Repayment of capital contributions (includes $1,378 working surplus)	$ 72,000	$ 200	
Equity buildup—total $14,300 80/20% split	11,440	2,860	
To general partners as agreed		20,000	
Balance $75,880—80/20% split	60,704	15,176	
Distribution of cash proceeds	$144,144	$ 38,236	($182,380)
			—0—
Cash distribution	$144,144	$ 38,236	
Less working surplus	1,375	3	
	$142,769	$ 38,233	
Equity buildup—deduct	11,440	2,860	
1. Actual proceeds of sale	$131,329	$ 35,373	
COST OF PARTNER INTERESTS			
Capital contributions (less working surplus)	$ 70,625	$ 197	
Less adjusted depreciation	(15,540)	(3,885)	
2. Depreciated cost	$ 55,085	($ 3,688)*	
Subtract line 2 from line 1 TAXABLE CAPITAL GAIN	$ 76,244	$ 39,061	

Assumed: Property held four years, sold to produce above cash after pro-rations.

*This figure adds to proceeds of sale.

Exhibit 20-4, on distribution of proceeds of sale of 4000 Redbird Boulevard Associates, assumes the amount of $182,380 is the amount of cash to be distributed after pro-rations and expenses of the sale at approximately $280,000 sale price.

The total repayment of capital contributions, their share of equity buildup, the payment of $20,000 to general partners, and the division of the excess profit, 80 per cent to limited partners and 20 per cent to general partners, are all shown on Exhibit 20-4, as well as the total capital gain.

Exhibit 20-5 shows the repayment of capital contribution and equity buildup, as well as the share of cash distributed to a single limited partner.

Exhibit 20-6 shows the capital gain tax status for a single limited partner.

EXHIBIT 20-5

4000 REDBIRD BOULEVARD ASSOCIATES

Division of Profit
Limited Partner

RROCEEDS OF SALE for Limited ($9,000)

Partnership interest		$18,018
DISTRIBUTION OF PROCEEDS OF SALE		
Repayment of capital contribution	$ 9,000	
Payment—equity buildup	1,430	
Payment—1/8th × $60,704 cash	7,588	
TOTAL CASH DISTRIBUTION of PROCEEDS of SALE		($18,018)
		—0—

EXHIBIT 20-6

CAPITAL GAIN TAX STATUS

Limited Partner Interest

PROCEEDS OF SALE		$18,018
DEDUCT :		
Refund of share of working surplus	$ 172	
Cost of limited partner interest, $9,000 less $172	8,828	
Equity buildup	1,430	
Adjusted depreciation	(1,942)	$ 8,488
TAXABLE CAPITAL GAIN for limited partner		$ 9,530

Exhibit 20-7 shows a four-year summary of net income from the 4000 Redbird Boulevard building, including the accelerated depreciation as taken and the recapture of excess depreciation which came about because the property was not held for ten years.

This example is for the syndicator. The limited partner would not need such a report, since he got monthly and annual reports of income, which would be sufficient for him.

Exhibit 20-8 shows the payment to the partners of their share of the equity buildup, the "cash flow" which had been paid to them, and the amount of "tax shelter" which applied. The depreciation would have made the entire equity buildup tax free during the holding period.

EXHIBIT 20-7

4000 REDBIRD BOULEVARD BUILDING

Four-Year Summary of Income

NET INCOME CREDITED TO PARTNERS' ACCOUNTS

	Total	Limited Partners 80%	General Partners 20%
Net income—12/1/64–11/30/68	$58,732	$46,986	$11,746
Depreciation—12/1/64–11/30/68	24,116	19,293	4,823
Taxable *before sale*	$34,616	$27,693	$ 6,923
Recapture of excess depreciation	(4,691)	(3,753)	(938)
TOTAL TAXABLE INCOME *after sale*	$39,308	$31,447	$ 7,861

EXHIBIT 20-8

DISTRIBUTION OF "CASH FLOW"

	Total	Limited partners 80%	General partners 20%
Net income—12/1/64–11/30/68	$58,732	$46,986	$11,746
Equity buildup—(mortgage payoff)	14,300*	11,440*	2,860*
"Cash flow"	$44,432	$35,546	$ 8,886
LESS total taxable	39,308	31,447	7,861
"Tax shelter" on "cash flow" four years	$ 5,124	$ 4,099	$ 1,025

*All of equity buildup is "tax sheltered."

Exhibit 20-9 is a four-year summary of income from the operation of the 4000 Red-bird Boulevard building which would apply to a single limited partner interest, showing this partner's total taxable income for the four years.

Exhibit 20-10—"Cash Flow" and Tax Status—also covers the interest of a single limited partner for the four years.

Exhibits 20-9 and 20-10 have been included for the benefit of the reader, to show how the deal would work out over the four-year period. The limited partners would have already had reports for the previous three years of operation of the property.

EXHIBIT 20-9

4000 REDBIRD BOULEVARD BUILDING

Four-Year Summary of Income
$9,000 Limited Partnership Interest

Net income—12/1/64–11/30/68	$5,873 Av. 16% + per annum
Depreciation	2,412
Taxable before sale	$3,461
Recapture of excess depreciation	469
TOTAL TAXABLE INCOME 12/1/64–11/30/68	$3,930

EXHIBIT 20-10

"CASH FLOW" and TAX STATUS

On Limited ($9,000) Partnership Interest—Four Years

Net income	$5,873
Equity buildup (mortgage payoff)	1,430*
"Cash flow"	$4,443 Av. 12% per annum
Taxable after sale	3,930
"Tax shelter" four years (only on "cash flow")	$ 513
NOTE: Total "tax shelter" includes all of equity buildup + part of "cash flow."	

*Equity buildup is "tax sheltered."

Exhibit 20-11 is a computation for a single limited partner, showing the consolidation of the income from operation of the property for the four-year period, and the capital gain which this partner would receive. This is an important report to make to a participating investor. Such a report of profit and capital gain would command the attention of any investor, and make him eager to join in another syndicate deal.

EXHIBIT 20-11

4000 REDBIRD BOULEVARD ASSOCIATES

*Summary of Four Years' Income Plus Capital Gain
Limited ($9,000) Interest*

Capital Contribution $ 9,000

Four Years' Operation of Property

"Cash Flow"	% Per Annum	Equity Buildup	Net Income	% per Annum	Depreci- ation	Taxable
$4,443	12% Av.	$1,430	$ 5,873	16% Av.	($1,942)	$ 3,930*
Capital Gain			7,588		add—1,942	9,530**
TOTAL INCOME FROM SYNDICATE			$13,461			$13,460

*Ordinary income—adjusted depreciation after sale
**Long term gain

Exhibit 20-12 is a computation of the division of profits and capital gain from the 4000 Redbird Boulevard Associates real estate syndicate, covering the interests of the general partners, the syndicators—John J. Jones and Samuel S. Smith.

Exhibit 20-13 is a summary of four years' income, plus capital gain and tax status, for one general partner interest.

Exhibit 20-14 shows the potential additional earnings which John J. Jones, a syndicator/ real estate broker, might make.

Prepare tax return for syndicate

The preparation of a syndicate income tax return for an income property would include the last year or portion of a year of operation of the property, and would also cover the sale of the syndicate property. This return should be prepared by the syndicate accountant as soon as possible after all transactions of the syndicate have been completed, and the organization dissolved. A copy of this income tax return should be supplied to each member of the syndicate group so that the participants can integrate the figures with their personal income tax returns.

EXHIBIT 20-12

4000 REDBIRD BOULEVARD ASSOCIATES

Division of Profit
General Partners

	John J. Jones 10%	Samuel S. Smith 10%
Proceeds of sale—1/2 each of $35,373	$17,686	$17,686
DISTRIBUTION OF PROCEEDS OF SALE		
Repayment of capital contribution	$ 100	$ 100
Payment equity buildup	1,430	1,430
Payment to general partners as agreed	10,000	10,000
Payment of 1/2 of $15,176	7,588	7,588
Total cash paid to general partners from proceeds of sale	$19,118	$19,118
Less working surplus contribution	(1)	(1)
	$19,117	$19,117
Deduct equity buildup	(1,430)	(1,430)
	$17,687	$17,687
Deduct cost each general partner interest	(99)	(99)
Add adjusted depreciation	1,942*	1,942*
TAXABLE CAPITAL GAIN—1/2 × $39,061	$19,530	$19,530

*Addition of depreciation taken makes capital gain exceed proceeds of sale.

EXHIBIT 20-13

4000 REDBIRD BOULEVARD ASSOCIATES

Summary of Four Years' Income Plus Capital Gain
One General Partner Interest

Capital contribution				$ 100

Four years' operation of property

"Cash Flow"	Equity Buildup	Net Income	Depreciation	Taxable
$4,443	$1,430	$ 5,873	($1,942)	$ 3,931*
Capital gain		17,588	add—1,942	19,530**
Total income from syndicate		$23,461		$23,461

*Ordinary income—adjusted depreciation after sale
**Long term gain

EXHIBIT 20-14

JOHN J. JONES—REAL ESTATE BROKER—GENERAL PARTNER

Total Income from Syndicate	$23,461
Management fee—four years—five percent × $104,000 collected	5,200
1/2 Commission on purchase of property	4,375
1/2 Commission on resale of property	7,000
Potential total income and capital gain from syndication	$40,036

Pay out all funds according to syndicate agreement and dissolve organization

An income property syndicate can usually be liquidated by first distributing the entire proceeds of the sale of the property to the various parties in interest, and their individual shares can be paid out of the sale escrow. The syndicator then uses the proceeds of the last month's operation of the property to pay any last bills due, including the cost of dissolving the organization. Thereafter he renders a final accounting and pays out the balance of the operating account to close the transaction.

POINTS TO KEEP IN MIND

√ Prepare an agenda for "Dividing the Profits" and closing out of a real estate syndicate transaction.

√ Provide all of the syndicate members with a copy of the agenda, as well as a copy of the sale contract or escrow agreement.

√ Arrange for the escrow company to divide the proceeds of the sale of syndicate property if possible.

√ Use working capital (or net rents from income property) to pay the final closing bills of the syndicate.

√ Render a complete report of the closing transactions to all of the members of the real estate syndicate, together with a syndicate income tax return, and make payment of any small balance of cash due each participant.

√ A prompt accounting by a syndicator, and a division of profits immediately after the organization is dissolved lays the foundation for the formation of another venture involving the same group of satisfied investors.

Index

A

Accountant, 38, 41-42
Accounting records, 178, 182
Acreage:
  development, 144
  holding period determinants, 149-151
    (see also Holding period)
  improvement, 143
  increasing value, 142-145
  leasing, 145
  natural resources, 145
  price increase, 142
  profit division (see Profit division)
  public improvements, 144-145
  rezoning, 143
  selling campaign, 166-170 (see also Selling campaign)
  selling price, 158-161 (see also Selling price)
  subdivision, 142-143
Acreage, syndication of:
  advantage to seller, 8
  advantages to purchasing, 8
  capital gain, 8-9
  determining value, 9
  disadvantages to purchasing, 8-9
  division, 9
  financing purchase, 8
  holding expenses, 8
  holding period, 9
  income, 8
  installment sale, 8-9
  management, 8-9, 123-125
    contract, 125
    fee, resolving, 124-125
    land manager, 125
    scope, 123-124
    selection of, 124
    type needed, 124
  prepaid interest, 8-9
  special influences on value, 8-9
  tax deductions, 8
  "tax shelter," 9
"Active market," 17-18
Advantages of syndication:
  acreage, 8
  real estate, improved, 13
  tax, 3, 5-6, 20
  vacant land, 7, 10-11
Advertising, 146, 169-170, 173

Agreement:
  organizational, 178, 181
  standard purchase, 109-111
  syndicate, 5-6, 33-34, 36, 78
Area development, 150, 155
Assessments, real estate, 18
Assessor's records:
  assessed valuation, 18
  disclose market activity, 18
  divulge property owner, 18
Attorney, selection of, 36, 38-41
Automobile parking, 148

B

Beneficiaries, 73
Bills, payment of, 43
"Box score," 18
Brochure, review of sample, 35
Broker:
  mortgage, 44-46
  real estate, 38, 42-43, 170, 173
Brokerage income, 4, 6, 15

C

California State Board of Equalization, 90
Capital for syndication, calculating, 15-16, 25-26
Capital gain potential:
  projecting, 120
  residential land, 11, 18-20
  urban land, 11, 17-20
Capital gain tax treatment, long term, 6
Capital gains, 3-6
Car parking, 148
Carrying charges, 11
"Cash flow," 12-13, 15, 18-19, 27-28, 84, 86, 90-91, 138, 148
Certificates of Joint Ventures, 79
Charges, carrying, 11
Classifications of real estate (see Real estate)
Clause, escalation, 45
Collection of rent, 43
Commercial vacant land, 10-12
Construction:
  financing, 12
  planning, 12
  supervising, 12
"Construction Spending," 95